The Look-It-Up Book of
PRESIDENTS

by Wyatt Blassingame

Random House  New York

For Philip Scott, who, like any American,
may be President someday.

Grateful acknowledgment is made to
Susan Semel and Carl Weiss for giving the
manuscript a careful historical reading.

Cover photographs and drawings courtesy: © Bettmann/CORBIS, front (J. Kennedy, G. Washington, A. Lincoln, T. Jefferson) and back cover; © Reuters NewMedia Inc./CORBIS (G. Bush); The White House.

Interior photographs and drawings courtesy of: Ankers Capitol Historical File, Capitol Photo Service Inc., p. 109; AP/Wide World Photos, pp. 96, 112, 131, 134, 135, 138, 139, 141, 142, 143, 152, 153, 154, 155, 156, 157, 158, 159, 166, 167, 168, 169, 170, 171, 173; © Bettmann/CORBIS, pp. 101, 102, 105, 115, 119, 121 (top), 122, 124, 126, 127, 146, 148; Brown Brothers, p. 48; George Bush Presidential Library, pp. 161, 162, 163, 164, 165; Chicago Historical Society, pp. 41 (ICHi–12739), 108 (ICHi–05601); Clinton family, p. 151; © CORBIS, p. 121 (bottom); George Eastman House/Lewis Wickes Hine, pp. 74, 79; Frederic Remington Art Museum, Ogdensburg, New York, p. 86; © Ewing Galloway, Inc., all rights reserved, pp. 16 (right), 21 (right), 123; Library of Congress, pp. 12, 19, 26, 33, 36, 38, 47, 56, 59, 61, 63, 66, 68, 70, 78, 84, 91, 111, 138; Metropolitan Museum of Art, Gift of I. N. Phelps Stokes, Edward S. Hawes, Alice Mary Hawes, and Marion Augusta Hawes, 1937 (37.14.34), p. 32; Monticello/Thomas Jefferson Memorial Foundation, Inc., p. 23; NASA, p. 130; National Archives, pp. 104, 110; New-York Historical Society, pp. 37, 52; New York Public Library Picture Collection, p. 54; © Reuters NewMedia Inc./CORBIS, p.160; Smithsonian Institution, National Museum of American History, pp. 14, 15, 18, 43, 60, 67, 73, 76, 81, 89 (Gift of Mr. and Mrs. Kermit Roosevelt), 93, 95, 97, 99, 118; U.S. Army, p. 117; U.S. Naval Academy Museum, p. 27; The White House, p. 1.

Revised edition 2001
Copyright © 1968, 1984, 1990, 1993, 1996, 2001 by Random House, Inc. Copyright renewed 1996 by Random House, Inc. All rights reserved under International and Pan-American Copyright Conventions. Published in the United States by Random House, Inc., New York, and simultaneously in Canada by Random House of Canada Limited, Toronto. Originally published by Random House, Inc., 1968. Revised editions published in 1984, 1990, 1993, and 1996.

www.randomhouse.com/kids

Library of Congress Cataloging-in-Publication Data
Blassingame, Wyatt.   The look-it-up book of presidents.
Includes index.
SUMMARY: Brief biographies of the presidents of the United States from George Washington to the winner of the 2000 presidential election.
ISBN 0-679-80358-0 (trade) — ISBN 0-394-96839-5 (lib. bdg.)
1. Presidents—United States—Biography—Juvenile literature. [1. Presidents.]
I. Title. E176.8.B55 2001 973.09'92—dc21 [B] [920] 89-10519

Printed in the United States of America   January 2001   10 9 8 7 6 5 4 3 2 1
RANDOM HOUSE and colophon are registered trademarks of Random House, Inc.

Contents

Wyatt Blassingame never met a President of the United States and divided his votes evenly between Democratic and Republican candidates after he reached voting age. The son of two teachers, he was born in Demopolis, Alabama, and spent his early years in small Alabama towns, where his parents' collection of books often became the town library. After graduating from the University of Alabama, he worked as a reporter, served as a navy lieutenant during World War II, and made a career of writing. He wrote more than six hundred stories and magazine articles, four adult novels, and more than sixty children's books—mostly about American history and animals. Mr. Blassingame died in 1985.

THE PRESIDENT OF THE UNITED STATES

Who can be President? Any natural-born citizen of the United States who is over the age of thirty-five and has lived in the United States for fourteen years or more.

What does a President do? The President is the chief executive of the United States. According to the Constitution, he "shall take care that the laws be faithfully executed." From time to time, he informs Congress in his State of the Union message what has been done and what needs to be done.

Although he cannot force Congress to act, he can suggest a program for them to consider. And as leader of his political party, he can often see that that program is carried out, when his party has a majority of seats. He can also prevent Congress from acting by using the presidential veto.

The President plays the chief part in shaping foreign policy. With the Senate's approval, he makes treaties with other nations and appoints ambassadors. But he can also make executive agreements with other nations without approval of the Senate.

He nominates Cabinet members, Supreme Court justices, and many other high officials. These nominations must be approved by the Senate. However, he can fill thousands of other important posts under his own power.

The President is Commander in Chief of the Armed Forces and commissions officers in all branches of the service.

How is the President elected? The voters of each state choose a number of electors equal to the number of senators and representatives they have in Congress. The electoral college, made up of the electors from every state, then chooses the President by majority vote. The electors usually vote for the candidate supported by the voters of their state. When there are more than two presidential candidates and none gets a clear majority, Congress selects the President from the three candidates who received the most votes (see chart on p. 6 of the electoral votes per state).

How long is the President in office? The President is elected to a term of four years. Since Article XXII of the Constitution became effective, in 1951, no President may be elected to more than two terms.

When does the President take office? The new President takes office at noon on January 20 of the year following his election, on taking this oath of office:

"I do solemnly swear (or affirm) that I will faithfully execute the office of President of the United States, and will, to the best of my ability, preserve, protect, and defend the Constitution of the United States."

Electoral Votes per State

State	Votes	State	Votes
Alabama	9	Nebraska	5
Alaska	3	Nevada	4
Arizona	8	New Hampshire	4
Arkansas	6	New Jersey	15
California	54	New Mexico	5
Colorado	8	New York	33
Connecticut	8	North Carolina	14
Delaware	3	North Dakota	3
Florida	25	Ohio	21
Georgia	13	Oklahoma	8
Hawaii	4	Oregon	7
Idaho	4	Pennsylvania	23
Illinois	22	Rhode Island	4
Indiana	12	South Carolina	8
Iowa	7	South Dakota	3
Kansas	6	Tennessee	11
Kentucky	8	Texas	32
Louisiana	9	Utah	5
Maine	4	Vermont	3
Maryland	10	Virginia	13
Massachusetts	12	Washington	11
Michigan	18	Washington, D.C.	3
Minnesota	10	West Virginia	5
Mississippi	7	Wisconsin	11
Missouri	11	Wyoming	3
Montana	3		

THE PRESIDENTS AT A GLANCE

NAME	SERVED	ACHIEVEMENTS
1. GEORGE WASHINGTON	*1789–1797*	The first President, he determined in large measure what the job of President should be. Held the country together during its early days and gave it a chance to grow. Ranked by historians as a "great" President.
2. JOHN ADAMS	*1797–1801*	Saved his country from an unnecessary war. Ranked by historians as a "near great" President.
3. THOMAS JEFFERSON	*1801–1809*	Bought the Louisiana Territory and doubled the size of the country. Made sure the government stayed in the hands of the people. Ranked by historians as a "great" or "near great" President.
4. JAMES MADISON	*1809–1817*	Allowed the country to get into unnecessary war, but made peace as quickly as possible. Ranked by historians as an "average" President.
5. JAMES MONROE	*1817–1825*	Took Florida from Spain. Created the Monroe Doctrine. Signed the Missouri Compromise. Ranked as one of the best of the "average" Presidents.
6. JOHN QUINCY ADAMS	*1825–1829*	Rated by some historians as a failure because little was done during his term. Some historians rank him as "average."
7. ANDREW JACKSON	*1829–1837*	Did more to show how great the powers of the office were than any President after Washington. Used these powers to help make laws. Ranked by historians as a "great" or "near great" President.
8. MARTIN VAN BUREN	*1837–1841*	Was caught in one of the nation's worst financial depressions. This was unfairly blamed on him. Ranked by historians as an "average" President.
9. WILLIAM HENRY HARRISON	*1841*	Was President for only one month.
10. JOHN TYLER	*1841–1845*	Made clear that on the death of a President the Vice President became President with all the powers of the office. Served as a President without a party. Ranked by most historians as "below average."
11. JAMES KNOX POLK	*1845–1849*	Bullied a small, weak nation (Mexico) into fighting a war it did not want, but added California and much of the Southwest to the United States. Settled the Canadian border without war. Ranked by historians as a "near great" President.
12. ZACHARY TAYLOR	*1849–1850*	Knew little about the duties of a President but faced his problems honestly though with little political talent. Served only two years. Ranked by many historians as "below average."
13. MILLARD FILLMORE	*1850–1853*	Sent the U.S. fleet to open trade with Japan. Helped pass the Great Compromise of 1850. Ranked by historians as "below average."
14. FRANKLIN PIERCE	*1853–1857*	Put through the Gadsden Purchase acquiring what is now southern Arizona and New Mexico. Favored the Kansas-Nebraska Act, which opened the door to the Civil War. Ranked by historians as "below average."
15. JAMES BUCHANAN	*1857–1861*	Faced the final breakup of the nation over slavery. Tried hard to prevent war but made matters worse instead of better. Ranked by historians as "below average."
16. ABRAHAM LINCOLN	*1861–1865*	Held the nation together in its most difficult time. In a speech at the Gettysburg battlefield he said it was the people's duty to make sure "that this nation, under God, shall have a new birth of freedom; and that government of the people, by the people, for the people, shall not perish from the earth." More than any other one man, he helped make these words come true. Ranked by historians as a truly "great" President.

17. ANDREW JOHNSON	*1865–1869*	Took office in a time of great trouble. Fought for what he believed was right, but did not have the power to persuade and lead men. Was impeached by Congress and came within one vote of being removed from office. Ranked by historians from "near great" to "below average."
18. ULYSSES SIMPSON GRANT	*1869–1877*	Was personally honest, but many of the men around him were crooks. His administration was one of the most dishonest in American history. One of the two Presidents rated as a "failure."
19. RUTHERFORD BIRCHARD HAYES	*1877–1881*	Ended the period of Reconstruction. Tried to reform the federal government after the Grant administration. Tried to improve the civil service system, but met with little success. Ranked by historians as "average."
20. JAMES ABRAM GARFIELD	*1881*	Was killed only a few months after taking office. Yet his death may have done more to improve honesty in government than he could have done had he lived.
21. CHESTER ALAN ARTHUR	*1881–1885*	Helped pass the first effective civil service laws and administered them honestly. Helped develop a modern navy. Ranked by historians as "average."
22. GROVER CLEVELAND & 24.	*1885–1889 and 1893–1897*	Made needed reforms in the federal government. Helped restore the confidence of the people in their government. His intentions were always good, but his methods sometimes failed. Ranked by historians as a "near great" President.
23. BENJAMIN HARRISON	*1889–1893*	Favored a strong foreign policy. Enlarged the navy. Wanted a better civil service, but Congress continually opposed him. Ranked by historians as "average."
25. WILLIAM McKINLEY	*1897–1901*	Allowed the United States to be pushed into war with Spain, but made the United States a world power. Acquired the Philippines, Hawaii, Guam, and Puerto Rico as United States possessions. Ranked by historians as "average."
26. THEODORE ROOSEVELT	*1901–1909*	Brought tremendous energy and vitality to the office of President. Used the powers of his office to control the power of huge business concerns. Worked to establish national parks and forests and the Panama Canal. Ranked by historians as one of the "near great" Presidents.
27. WILLIAM HOWARD TAFT	*1909–1913*	Worked hard for conservation of natural resources. Helped improve the Post Office system. Fought to break the power of the trusts. Ranked by historians as "average."
28. WOODROW WILSON	*1913–1921*	Reformed the banking laws. Worked to improve the antitrust laws, to help the American worker, and to lower the tariff. Tried to stay out of World War I, then tried hard to make it a "war to end all wars." Worked for a League of Nations to keep the world at peace. Failed, but left an ideal of which people still dream. Ranked by historians as a "great" President.
29. WARREN GAMALIEL HARDING	*1921–1923*	In large measure let Congress and his Cabinet run the nation. Was more loyal to his friends than to his country. His was probably the most dishonest administration in United States history. Ranked by historians as a "failure."
30. CALVIN COOLIDGE	*1923–1929*	Believed the powers of the President should be very limited and that government should leave business alone. Took very little action but restored honesty and dignity to the presidency. Ranked by historians as "below average."
31. HERBERT HOOVER	*1929–1933*	Saw the country plunged into its worst financial depression and was unfairly blamed for it. Tried to improve business, but his efforts were not enough. Ranked by historians as "average."
32. FRANKLIN DELANO ROOSEVELT	*1933–1945*	Saw the United States through two grave crises: the Great Depression of the 1930s and World War II. Promoted laws that changed the course of American government. Ranked by historians as a "great" President.

33.	**HARRY S. TRUMAN**	*1945–1953*	Was faced by important decisions and made most of them correctly. Established the Truman Doctrine, by which the United States would help other nations trying to stay free of Communist control. Worked for social welfare and civil rights laws. Ranked by most historians as a "near great" President.
34.	**DWIGHT DAVID EISENHOWER**	*1953–1961*	Ended the war in Korea. Tried to lessen troubles with the Soviet Union. Sent troops to Little Rock, Arkansas, to enforce school integration. Ranked by most historians as "average."
35.	**JOHN FITZGERALD KENNEDY**	*1961–1963*	Worked for equal rights for all citizens. Established the Peace Corps. Forced the Soviet Union to withdraw its missiles from Cuba.
36.	**LYNDON BAINES JOHNSON**	*1963–1969*	Pushed more important laws through Congress than any President since Franklin Roosevelt, including civil rights and antipoverty measures. Tried unsuccessfully to make peace in Vietnam.
37.	**RICHARD MILHOUS NIXON**	*1969–1974*	Ended U.S. military involvement in Vietnam. Opened relations with Communist China. His administration was caught in one of the worst political scandals in American history.
38.	**GERALD RUDOLPH FORD**	*1974–1977*	His fair and open administration helped to heal the wounds of Watergate. Improved relations with China. Was the first person to occupy the White House without having been elected either President or Vice President.
39.	**JIMMY (JAMES EARL) CARTER**	*1977–1981*	Helped bring about a peace treaty between Israel and Egypt. Improved relations with Latin America by giving control of the Panama Canal to Panama. Worked to improve human rights throughout the world.
40.	**RONALD WILSON REAGAN**	*1981–1989*	Built up U.S. military power. Worked to reduce inflation and led the fight to reduce taxes. The national debt increased massively during his administration. In his second term, he began arms-limitation talks with Soviet leader Mikhail Gorbachev.
41.	**GEORGE HERBERT WALKER BUSH**	*1989–1993*	His election marked the 200th anniversary of the U.S. Presidency. Presided during the breakup of the Soviet Union and the fall of Communist rule in Eastern Europe. In the Persian Gulf War, led a coalition of nations in driving the Iraqi army out of Kuwait.
42.	**BILL (WILLIAM JEFFERSON BLYTHE) CLINTON**	*1993–2001*	The first President born after World War II, he took office at the end of the Cold War and shifted American priorities from maintaining military power to strengthening U.S. economic clout. The second President to be impeached (for lying under oath about a sexual affair and then trying to hamper an investigation), he presided over the longest period of economic prosperity in the nation's history.
43.	**GEORGE WALKER BUSH**	*2001–*	The fourth man in American history to become President despite losing the popular vote, he's also the second to follow in his father's footsteps by winning the White House (John Quincy Adams was the first). His election avenged his father's defeat and returned the Republican Party to the White House after an eight-year exile.

GEORGE WASHINGTON

1st President of the United States, 1789–1797

Born: February 22, 1732, near Fredericksburg, Virginia
Died: December 14, 1799, at Mount Vernon, Virginia

April 30, 1789. General George Washington stood on the balcony of Federal Hall in New York City. Around him were many of the greatest men in America. In the street below, a huge crowd stood quietly.

Slowly, solemnly, Washington took the oath that made him the first President of the United States. He leaned forward and kissed the Bible on which he had sworn. Then from the men on the balcony and from the street below a great roar went up. "Long live George Washington, President of the United States!" Everyone was sure they had chosen their best leader to be the first President.

But what was the job of the President? Was he to be a dictator who would run the country to suit himself? Was he to be a figurehead who would sign laws that Congress passed? The answers lay in the hands of the tall man on the balcony. He would shape the job, and with it the future of the new nation.

Washington realized this. He once said, "I walk on untrodden ground. There is scarcely any part of my conduct that may not hereafter be drawn into precedent."

Washington's father was a well-to-do farmer. The boy spent much of his time outdoors. He grew tall and lean with fair skin that sunburned easily. He became an excellent horseman. He went to school only off and on, and only until he was about fifteen. But he was always good at figures. At fourteen he surveyed his father's farms just for fun. (Surveyors determine the exact boundaries of a piece of land.)

At fifteen George went with a party of surveyors to work in the Shenandoah Valley. Later he worked for a time as public surveyor of Fairfax County, Virginia. Then, when he was twenty-one years old, his military life began.

George Washington is sworn in as the first President of the United States on the balcony of Federal Hall in New York City on April 30, 1789.

At this time the American Colonies still belonged to England. Canada belonged to France. French soldiers from Canada had built forts in the Ohio Valley on land claimed by England. The governor of Virginia appointed young Washington to ride through the wilderness and tell the French they would have to leave.

One French fort was near what is now Waterford, Pennsylvania. Here the French commander greeted Washington politely but said that the Ohio Valley belonged to France and that the French soldiers would not leave.

A year later British General Edward Braddock led a small army against the French and the Indians (now known as Native Americans). Washington was Braddock's aide-de-camp. The British general knew nothing about fighting in the wilderness. His troops marched straight into an ambush and were badly defeated. But in the fighting Washington showed the qualities of a first-rate officer. He had a cool, thoughtful courage. He was not hurt, but two horses were killed under him and his uniform was slashed by four bullets. It was largely due to his leadership that part of the British Army escaped.

After this battle Washington was made commander of all the Virginia troops. For several years he led them in small frontier fights against the French and the Indians. Then, when he was twenty-six years old, he quit the army. He had met a rich young widow named Martha Dandridge Custis. He married her and settled down.

For the next fifteen years Washington spent most of his time at his farm called Mount Vernon. He was a wealthy tobacco planter. Like most other successful planters, Washington was a slave owner. He raised horses and cattle, apples, peaches, and pears. This was one of the happiest times in his life. He had no children of his own, but he loved the little girl and boy who were Martha's children by her first husband.

At this time great changes were taking place in the American Colonies. The Colonies still belonged to England, but many Americans thought they were not being treated fairly. They thought the Colonies should have more to say about their own government. At last the quarrel grew into a war.

On April 19, 1775, British soldiers clashed with Americans at Lexington and Concord. The Revolutionary War began. Because of his military experience, George Washington was appointed commander in chief of the American army. The fact that he was a southerner was very important. Most of the army outside Boston was Yankee, and Congress wanted a general who would attract southerners to join. Congress also wanted a wealthy man as general, since they could not afford to pay him.

Today most military experts believe that George Washington was a good general but not a great one. His army lost more battles than it won. But it was never destroyed. It was never captured. Washington himself said that as long as the Americans could keep an army in the field, the British could not win. And somehow Washington kept his army in the field. This was where he was truly great. He had an unusual ability to inspire men. His soldiers did not have enough guns or enough ammunition. They were often ragged and hungry. Washington lived and suffered with them. And in some way he made them feel that as long as he led them they could not lose. By the sheer strength of his character he held his army together. He kept it fighting.

At this time France also was at war with England. With the help of a French fleet, American soldiers trapped a British army under Lord Cornwallis at Yorktown, Virginia. On October 21, 1781, Cornwallis surrendered. The peace treaty was not signed for almost two years, but Yorktown was the end of the actual fighting. The Colonies had won. Now they were free and independent states.

During the war American soldiers had been poorly paid. After the war they expected some reward from Congress, but Congress was slow to act. The soldiers became angry. Some of them wanted Washington to lead a revolt and make himself king. He could easily have done so. But Washington refused to turn against his own government. He refused to be king. Once more he quit the army and went back to his home at Mount Vernon.

Washington was happiest at home with his family. But soon the new nation was in trouble. Each of the states considered itself independent. There was danger they might start fighting among themselves.

In the summer of 1787 men from the different states met in Philadelphia to try to draw up plans for a new government. The meeting was called the Constitutional Convention. Many of the most important men in Amer-

The first flag of the United States

ica were there. George Washington was elected chairman of the convention. His job was to hold the convention together as he had held his army together. All summer he kept these men working.

The plan they finally drew up was the Constitution of the United States. With some changes it is the same basic plan by which we are governed today. It called for a strong central government headed by a President. George Washington was elected the first President. He received every vote.

Washington did not believe in government by political parties. He thought his job was to be President of all the people, and he appointed to his Cabinet the best men he could find. These men, however, did not always agree with Washington, and they did not always agree with one another. Alexander Hamilton, secretary of the treasury, wanted a very strong central government run only by men who were both rich and intelligent. Thomas Jefferson, secretary of state, believed that most powers should belong to the states. And he had more faith in the people than Hamilton did.

Political parties began to form around these two men. People who agreed with Hamilton were called Federalists. Those who agreed with Jefferson were called Republicans. (Much later this party would change its name to the Democratic party, and a new Republican party would be formed.)

With his great personal influence, Washington might have made himself dictator. He might have told Congress what laws to pass and what not to pass. On the other hand he might have left everything to Congress, if he had wished. Instead, he set a middle course. Some later Presidents have made the

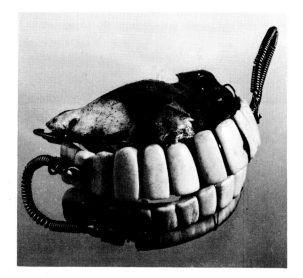

Washington's false teeth, which were made of ivory by John Greenwood in 1795

office of President stronger, some weaker. But all have been influenced by the course that Washington set.

Washington was not a brilliant man. Thomas Jefferson said Washington's mind "was slow in operation . . . but sure in conclusion." He never acted "until every circumstance, every consideration was maturely weighed . . . but when once decided upon, going through with his purpose whatever obstacles opposed."

Washington believed that as the chief officer of a new nation, he should present a dignified appearance, like the King of England—his only model at that time. So Washington dressed very formally. Whenever he traveled he went in a handsome carriage pulled by beautiful horses. He could laugh at jokes, but he rarely told any. He inspired awe rather than friendship, even in the great men around him.

In 1793 Washington was elected to a second term. Now the nation was facing new and ever more difficult problems.

France and England were at war again. Many Americans now wanted to help France. Washington wanted to keep his country at peace. The United States, he said, should stay out of European troubles.

More trouble came when the federal government placed a tax on whiskey. Many people did not believe that the federal government had the right to tax individuals in that way. They refused to pay. In what was called the Whiskey Rebellion, government tax collectors in Washington County, Pennsylvania, were badly beaten. The governor of Pennsylvania refused to punish the rebels.

Washington knew that no government could last unless it had the power to enforce its laws on individuals. He sent troops into Pennsylvania and put down the rebellion. He proved that the federal government could enforce its laws.

Now for the first time a number of people began to complain about Washington. Even so, most people wanted

him to be President for a third term. But he was sixty-five years old. He was tired. He refused a third term and went back to the life he loved at Mount Vernon.

He did not enjoy it for long. On December 12, 1799, he was caught in a snowstorm while riding around his farm and became sick. Two days later he died.

The news of his death came as a great shock to the whole world. Even the British, whom he had fought, had learned to admire and respect him. Thomas Jefferson, who often disagreed with Washington, said, "He was indeed, in every sense of the words, a wise, a good, and a great man." But it was one of Washington's old soldiers who put the nation's feelings into words. Washington, said General Lighthorse Harry Lee, was "first in war, first in peace, and first in the hearts of his countrymen."

JOHN ADAMS

2nd President of the United States, 1797–1801

Born: October 30, 1735, in Braintree (now Quincy), Massachusetts
Died: July 4, 1826, in Braintree, Massachusetts

John Adams was born on a small farm near what is now Quincy, Massachusetts. His parents were not well educated, but they sent John to Harvard University. Afterward he taught school briefly, then studied law. He was still studying law when he heard a speech that influenced the rest of his life.

The speech was made in 1761 by a man named James Otis. The American Colonies still belonged to England. Otis was speaking against a law passed by the British Parliament. Otis said the law was unfair because the Colonies had no one in Parliament to speak against it. If a law was unfair and unjust, the people had a right to oppose it. They had a right to make their own laws.

Young Adams was deeply moved. Liberty—the freedom to make one's own laws—it was for this that Adams's ancestors had emigrated to America. And liberty was what he be-

lieved in with his whole heart.

Adams became one of the leaders in the American independence movement. From 1774 to 1778 he was a member of the Continental Congress. He was there on June 7, 1776, when Richard Henry Lee of Virginia moved "that the united Colonies are, and of right ought to be, free and independent States."

Adams was a member of the committee appointed to write the Declaration of Independence. Thomas Jefferson did most of the actual writing; but it was Adams who led the debate in Congress to have the declaration passed.

In 1778 Adams wrote a constitution for his home state of Massachusetts. Later it would serve as one of the models for the Constitution of the United States.

During the Revolutionary War, Adams worked for his country in Europe.

Two mugs commemorating the presidential campaign of John Adams

He was one of the men who drew up the final peace treaty with England. After that he served as the United States ambassador to England.

In 1789, when George Washington was elected the first President, Adams was elected Vice President. He was not happy in his new job. He liked to talk, but as Vice President, he had to be quiet while others talked. Once he wrote his wife that the job of Vice President was "the most insignificant office that ever the invention of man contrived."

In 1797, when George Washington refused a third term, Adams was elected President. Thomas Jefferson was elected Vice President. Like Washington, Adams did not believe in political parties. He thought of the President as a "patriot king" and not as the leader of one party. But political parties had already been formed. And Adams soon found himself in trouble.

The Federalist party, led by Alexander Hamilton, believed in government by a small group of rich and powerful men. The Republican party (which later changed its name to the Democratic party) believed in government by the mass of people. Adams stood somewhere in the middle, but he had been elected by the Federalists.

Adams was a good lawyer and a very smart man. But he was not a good politician. He was proud and stubborn. Also, he was a poor judge of men. All the men he appointed to his Cabinet were Federalists. They were more loyal to Hamilton, the leader of the party, than to Adams. Hamilton was not a member of the government, but for a while he seemed to be more powerful than the President.

At this time France was at war with England and other European countries. Hamilton wanted the United States to have close ties with England even if it meant war with France. Adams, like Washington, did not want the United States closely tied with any

European country. Also, he wanted peace if possible. He sent men to talk with the French government.

The French refused to talk with the Americans unless the United States paid them money. Adams wanted peace, but not at any price. He would not pay a bribe to France. Instead, he asked Congress to order new warships. A navy department was established for the first time. Adams is sometimes called the Father of the United States Navy. There was no declaration of war, but American and French warships fought whenever they met.

The Federalists wanted war with France. Against the wishes of Hamilton and his Cabinet, Adams sent more men to France to talk peace. This time the French government was willing to meet with them, and a war that might have destroyed the young nation was avoided.

Near the end of Adams's term as President, the government moved from Philadelphia to the new capital city of Washington, D.C. The unfinished White House was cold and damp. But on his second night in the White House, Adams wrote: "I pray Heaven to bestow the best Blessings on this House and all that shall hereafter inhabit it. May none but honest and wise men ever rule beneath this roof."

In saving his country from war, Adams had angered the leaders of the Federalist party. In the election of 1801 they turned against him and he was defeated. He went back to his home in Massachusetts. He died there on July 4, 1826, exactly fifty years after the Declaration of Independence.

Adams was a true patriot as well as a brave and stubborn man. Before his death he asked that the words on his tomb read: "Here lies John Adams, who took upon himself the responsibility of the peace with France in the year 1800."

The original Capitol building in Washington, D.C., as it looked in 1800. At that time the city's population was only 3,210.

THOMAS JEFFERSON

3rd President of the United States, 1801–1809

*Born: April 13, 1743, in Goochland (now Albemarle) County, Virginia
Died: July 4, 1826, in Charlottesville, Virginia*

When Thomas Jefferson was born, Goochland County was still frontier country. Peter Jefferson, Thomas's father, was a moderately well-to-do farmer and surveyor there. Thomas's mother came from one of the best families in Virginia.

Jefferson was tall and thin with a freckled face and sandy hair. He had one of the most brilliant minds in American history. Before he was thirty years old he had studied half a dozen languages, law, mathematics, science, and philosophy. He was a self-taught architect who designed some of the most beautiful homes in the world. He was an inventor. He invented the American system of money. He was a fine musician.

When he was twenty-six years old, Jefferson was elected to the Virginia legislature. Surprisingly, he was not a good public speaker, so instead of making speeches he wrote many let-

ters and articles. Often these were about the growing trouble between the Colonies and Great Britain. One of his articles was about what Jefferson called "The Rights of America." It made Jefferson's name known in all the Colonies. His opposition to England became so strong that the British declared him a traitor to be hanged once he was seized.

In 1772 he married Martha Skelton. Three years later he was elected to the Continental Congress. Because of his fame as a writer, he was appointed to write the Declaration of Independence.

During the Revolutionary War, Jefferson was first a member of the Virginia legislature, then governor of the state. He worked hard to pass a law guaranteeing freedom of religion. It was the first law of its kind in America.

After the war Jefferson served as minister to France. Then, when the new Constitution was adopted and Washington was elected President, Jefferson was appointed secretary of state.

From the first, Jefferson was afraid that the United States might someday become a dictatorship. He believed with all his heart that the people should, and could, govern themselves. Raised on the frontier, Jefferson hoped America would become a nation of farmers needing few laws. He believed only educated citizens could safeguard the new democracy. And so he thought all children should have to go to school through the third grade. To us this doesn't seem like much education, but in Jefferson's time many people had no schooling at all.

Alexander Hamilton, Washington's secretary of the treasury, loved his country as much as Jefferson did. But he did not agree with Jefferson's ideas of what made a good government. He believed that the English system, headed by a king or at least a lifetime President, would be best. Each man honestly believed he was right. But Jefferson believed that Hamilton's ideas would turn the United States into a dictatorship. And Hamilton thought Jefferson's ideas would end in mob rule.

Jefferson did not, at first, intend to form a political party. But soon he became the leader of the men who agreed with him. They began to be called Republicans. (Years later the Republicans began to call themselves Democrats.) The men who agreed with Hamilton became known as Federalists. Nobody planned it, but this was the beginning of the party system in the United States.

President Washington agreed more often with Hamilton than with Jefferson. At the end of Washington's first term Jefferson resigned and went back to Virginia.

When Washington refused to serve a third term, John Adams was elected President and Thomas Jefferson was elected Vice President. Adams belonged to the Federalist party, Jefferson to the Republican party. This mixup happened because the men who wrote the Constitution had not thought about political parties. They planned for the man who got the most votes to be President and for the man who got the second most votes to be Vice President. Later the Constitution would be changed so that the President and Vice President would always belong to the same party.

Adams served only one term, then Jefferson was elected President. Because he believed the country should

be run as cheaply as possible, he cut down on the army and navy. He did not wear handsome uniforms, as Washington had done. Nor did he ride in a big carriage pulled by many horses. Instead he walked or rode horseback.

At this time France claimed most of the vast, unknown land west of the Mississippi River. At New Orleans, France controlled the land on both sides of the river. This meant France could close the river to American boats if it wanted to. But this river traffic was very important to American settlers west of the Appalachian Mountains. So in 1803 Jefferson tried to buy New Orleans from France. To his surprise, Napoleon, the French emperor, offered to sell the whole Louisiana Territory, from the Mississippi River to the Rocky Mountains.

Jefferson believed that a President had no powers except those put down in the Constitution. And nothing in the Constitution said a President could double the size of the United States. But Jefferson also believed that the future of the United States lay in the west. Here was too good a chance for his country to miss. He signed the treaty buying the Louisiana Territory. Then he asked Congress for permission to do what he had already done. Some people were angry at Jefferson for doing more than the Constitution said he could. Others said he was trying to make himself emperor of the vast new territory.

About this time there was also trouble with the Barbary pirates, who lived along the northern coast of Africa. For a number of years their warships had been capturing American merchant ships in the Mediterranean Sea and holding the crews for ransom. It was cheaper to pay than to fight, but Jefferson would not take this way out. He sent the tiny U.S. Navy to attack the pirates. After defeating the pirates in several sea battles, the navy finally forced them to let American ships pass through the Mediterranean in peace.

In 1804 Jefferson was elected for a second term.

France and England were at war again. English warships often captured American merchant ships to keep them from trading with France. To avoid war, Jefferson got Congress to pass a law forbidding American ships to trade with either England or France. English trade, however, was big business in the New England states. Merchants began to lose money. After a while Jefferson realized the law was doing his country more harm than good. One of his last acts as President was to ask Congress to repeal the unpopular law.

Jefferson might have been elected again if he had wished. But he was always afraid that if a President served for too long, he might be tempted to become a dictator. Jefferson did not believe that any man should be President for more than two terms. Also, he had never been really happy as President. So he refused to be elected for a third term. He went back to his beautiful home called Monticello and to his life as a planter. Like other southern planters (including George Washington), Jefferson was a slave owner. He was troubled by slavery and in his will he freed some of his slaves. He did not free them while he was alive because he did not want to seem to be criticizing his slave-owning neighbors. Evidence points to Jefferson's having had a long-term, close relationship with his slave Sally Hemings, who is said to have borne his children.

Jefferson's service to his country was not yet over. He planned and helped build the University of Virginia. He brought together the teachers and helped decide what subjects should be taught. And he gave advice to later Presidents of the United States.

Jefferson's home, which sits on a hill overlooking Charlottesville, Virginia. He designed it himself and called it Monticello, or "little mountain." Bottom left: the parlor, whose parquet floor was designed by Jefferson (the first of its kind in the New World). Bottom right: the dining room.

Thomas Jefferson died on the same day as John Adams, July 4, 1826. It was exactly fifty years after the Declaration of Independence, which he had written. Jefferson wrote the words to go on his gravestone: "Here was buried Thomas Jefferson, author of the Declaration of Independence, of the statute of Virginia for religious freedom, and father of the University of Virginia."

He did not even mention having been President of the United States.

JAMES MADISON

4th President of the United States, 1809–1817

Born: March 16, 1751, in Port Conway, Virginia
Died: June 28, 1836, in Montpelier, Virginia

Most of James Madison's youth was spent in Orange County, Virginia. He was a thin, sickly child. He had all his lessons at home until he was eighteen. He never weighed much more than a hundred pounds and he was only five and a half feet tall.

When he was a teenager his health improved and he went to Princeton University, where he often studied for sixteen and seventeen hours a day. Even so, he had some time to take part in the long talks between students and teachers. Many of the discussions dealt with the growing troubles between the American Colonies and Great Britain. Madison was always on the side of the Colonies.

It took Madison only two years to graduate from Princeton. For a while he thought about being a preacher. He was sincerely religious and he believed deeply in religious freedom. Religion and government, he thought, ought to be kept completely separate.

But instead of going into the church, young Madison went into politics. During the Revolution he served in the Continental Congress. After the war was over he was one of the first men to recognize the great problems facing the new country.

At this time the nation had no real central government. Each state considered itself more or less independent. Madison knew that if the country was to get along, it must have a central government with more power. He and other leaders urged that a convention be called to form such a government.

This convention met in Philadelphia in the summer of 1787. Madison was one of the members and prime movers. Later another member of the convention wrote about Madison: "Every person seems to acknowledge his greatness. . . . In the management of every question he . . . took the lead."

The plan finally settled on became the Constitution of the United States. With some changes it is the same plan by which we are governed today. Madison is often called the Father of the Constitution.

When the new government was formed, Madison was elected to the House of Representatives. There he led the fight to add the first ten amendments to the Constitution. These are known today as the Bill of Rights.

Madison did not get married until he was forty-three years old. He was sixteen years older than his bride, Dolley Todd. They were an odd-looking couple—the young, laughing, pretty girl and the thin, sick-looking, middle-aged man. And yet they were a very happy couple.

In 1801 Thomas Jefferson appointed Madison secretary of state. For eight years the two men worked closely together. When Jefferson retired, Madison was elected President as a Republican.

France and England were still at war

Dolley Payne Todd Madison. She is remembered for rescuing important state papers and a portrait of George Washington when the British set the White House on fire in August 1814.

The U.S.S. *Constitution* (later called Old Ironsides) bombards the British ship *Guerrière* near Nova Scotia during the War of 1812.

with each other. Whenever possible England captured American ships to keep them from trading with France. And France captured American ships to keep them from trading with England.

Some of the young men in the Republican party wanted a war with England. Madison could not control them. Although he had a brilliant mind, he was not a great leader of men.

The War Hawks, as these young men were called, were using the British attacks on American ships only as an excuse. What they really wanted was to capture Canada from England and Florida from Spain, which was an ally of England. In June 1812 they talked Madison into asking Congress to declare war on England. This was called the War of 1812.

The war was not popular with ship owners, most of whom lived in New England. They called it Mr. Madison's War. The war was supposed to protect their shipping. Actually it kept them from trading and making money. Also, many of the ship owners belonged to the Federalist party.

At first things went badly for the United States. American armies were defeated along the Canadian border. American ships won a few brilliant victories, but they could not stand up to the big British fleet. The city of Washington was captured by the English, who burned the White House and the Capitol building. Then the British fleet sailed up the Chesapeake Bay to attack Baltimore. But they were turned back there. And an American lawyer named Francis Scott Key, who watched the battle, wrote "The Star-Spangled Banner."

Madison had begun peace talks with the English almost as soon as he began the war. Finally in 1815 a peace treaty was signed in Europe. The news took so long to reach the United States that the final battle was actually fought after peace had been declared. This was the Battle of New Orleans—the Americans, under General Andrew Jackson, won a smashing victory.

The peace treaty settled none of the problems that had caused the war. But because of Jackson's victory over the British at New Orleans most Americans felt they had won the war.

At the end of his second term Madison was glad to retire and go back to his home in Virginia. He had done his best as President. But his greatest achievement was masterminding the writing of the Constitution.

Dolley Madison was also famous in her own right as a gracious hostess. She was one of the best loved of all the First Ladies. After her husband's death she returned to the capital and again took up her position as the leading lady of Washington society. After a full and eventful life she died at the age of eighty-one.

JAMES MONROE

5th President of the United States, 1817–1825

Born: April 28, 1758, in Westmoreland County, Virginia
Died: July 4, 1831, in New York, New York

James Monroe was the last of the Revolutionary leaders to become President. Like all the Presidents before him except John Adams, he was born in Virginia. He was tall and rawboned and had a quiet, natural dignity. When he was sixteen, Monroe left home to go to William and Mary College. Two years later, in 1776, he left college to join the Revolutionary Army.

After the war Monroe studied law under Thomas Jefferson. Although Jefferson was fifteen years older, the two men became close friends. When Monroe was only twenty-four, he was elected to the Virginia legislature. Later he served in the U.S. Senate and then as governor of Virginia.

In 1811 President James Madison appointed Monroe secretary of state. In fact, for a while during the War of 1812, Monroe was both secretary of state and secretary of war.

In 1816 he was elected President. By then the War of 1812 was over. The Federalist party, which had opposed Monroe, had not helped to fight the war and was no longer popular. To find out how the people did feel and what they wanted, Monroe went on a trip across the country. Although styles had changed, he still wore old-fashioned knee breeches and shoes with buckles on them. People remembered that he had been an officer in the Revolution and wounded in battle. Everywhere he went he was met by cheering crowds. In Boston a newspaper wrote this was the "era of good feeling." Soon the time of Monroe's presidency came to be known as the Era of Good Feeling.

Even though the war was over, both the United States and Great Britain still had warships on the Great Lakes. There was always a chance that fighting might start again. Monroe suggested that each country limit its warships on the lakes to a few very small ones.

England agreed. That set up a spirit of friendly cooperation and peaceful negotiation that still exists among Britain, the United States, and Canada today.

At this time Florida still belonged to Spain. But there were only a few Spanish settlers in Florida. American settlers in Georgia looked at the open land to the south and wanted it.

Seminoles from Florida sometimes raided the Georgia farms. The Spanish government was not strong enough to stop them. So President Monroe sent General Andrew Jackson with a small army to fight the Seminoles. Jackson did not find many Seminoles. But he did capture the city of Pensacola from the Spanish, even though the United States was not at war with Spain.

President Monroe ordered Jackson to withdraw his troops, but it was clear the United States could capture Florida at any time. So the two governments signed a treaty by which Spain gave Florida to the United States. In return the United States gave up its claim to have bought Texas as part of the Louisiana Purchase.

In 1820 Monroe was elected to a second term. He got every vote in the electoral college except one. The one man who voted against Monroe said he did not think anybody but Washington should ever get all the votes.

Until about the time of Monroe's first election, Spain had claimed most of South and Central America. But as Spain grew weak one South American country after another declared its independence. Spain itself could not stop them. But in 1823 Spain asked the help of France and other European countries. Together they might reconquer the newly free countries of South America.

President Monroe did not like the idea. He declared that the United States did not want any European country meddling in American affairs. No new colonies were to be started in the Americas. This became known as the Monroe Doctrine. It has been a basic doctrine of the United States ever since.

When his second term was over, Monroe went back to his home in Virginia. He died while visiting his daughter in New York in 1831. The day was the Fourth of July. Of the five Presidents who took part in the Revolution, three of them—Thomas Jefferson, John Adams, and James Monroe—died on a Fourth of July.

JOHN QUINCY ADAMS

6th President of the United States, 1825–1829

Born: July 11, 1767, in Quincy, Massachusetts
Died: February 23, 1848, in the speaker's room in
the House of Representatives, Washington, D.C.

John Quincy Adams was seven years old when the Battle of Bunker Hill was fought. It was a day he would never forget. Already he loved his country with fierce pride.

John Quincy Adams was the son of John Adams, second President of the United States. He was the only son of a President to become President himself.

When John Quincy Adams was eleven years old, his father was sent to France as an American diplomat. He took John Quincy Adams with him. During the next few years the boy went to school in France and Germany. When he was only fourteen he went to Russia to serve as secretary for the American minister. The following year he worked as secretary for his father. At this time John Adams was helping write the peace treaty that ended the American Revolution.

When the fighting ended, John Quincy Adams went to Harvard University. He graduated in 1787, then studied law. But soon he was sent by President Washington to represent the United States in one European country after another.

When Thomas Jefferson became President, John Quincy Adams returned to the United States. A year later he was elected to the Senate as a member of the Federalist party. But Adams, like his father and George Washington, never believed in political parties. He voted for what he thought was right, whether the party liked it or not. Soon he began to agree with the Republican party more often than with the Federalists. As a result he lost his office after one term.

President Madison, a Republican, sent Adams to Europe in 1814. There he helped write the peace treaty that

A daguerreotype portrait of John Quincy Adams. This was an early form of photography that was invented in France in 1839.

ended the War of 1812. When James Monroe became President in 1817, he appointed Adams secretary of state.

Adams became one of the truly great secretaries of state. He was a short, heavyset man with heavy-lidded eyes and a cold mouth. He did not make many friends, but he made the best possible bargains for his country. He helped settle a quarrel between the United States and England over the Oregon Territory. He wrote the treaty by which the United States won Florida. He played a very important part in framing the Monroe Doctrine.

In the Presidential election of 1824 there were four important candidates. In the electoral college, Andrew Jackson got the most votes, Adams was second, but no one got a majority. This meant the final choice had to be made in the House of Representatives. Adams was chosen. It was an honest election, but Jackson and his followers were angry. They accused Adams of making crooked deals to win the election.

Adams's four years as President were

probably the most unhappy years of his life. He loved his country deeply, but he was a cold and harsh man. Many people admired his intelligence, but almost no one liked him. His sharp tongue made enemies. Yet as President, Adams chose not to defend himself. He said it was beneath the dignity of a President to answer the lies told about him. And Adams was lonely. In the early mornings he went for long walks by himself or swam in the Potomac River.

Adams wanted the United States to become a center of learning. He asked Congress to build a national university. He asked for roads and canals and a naval academy. Later most of these things would be done. But Adams could never get along with Congress. As a

The Erie Canal, which was completed while Adams was President. It took 8 years to finish the 365-mile waterway which connects Albany and Buffalo, New York.

result they refused to do what he asked. In the election of 1828 he was defeated and Andrew Jackson was elected.

Deeply hurt by his defeat, Adams went back to his home in Massachusetts. But then the people of his area elected him to Congress. Some people said he would be disgraced by serving in Congress after being President. Adams's answer was typical of him. He said that no man was disgraced by serving his country.

For the next seventeen years Adams served in Congress. He fought for the things he had always believed in. He helped establish the Smithsonian Institution. He fought against slavery and for civil rights and free speech. He was one of the nation's finest congressmen. He was at his desk on February 21, 1848, when he fell unconscious. Two days later he died.

ANDREW JACKSON

7th President of the United States, 1829–1837

Born: March 15, 1767, in the Waxhaw settlement (on the border of North Carolina), South Carolina
Died: June 8, 1845, near Nashville, Tennessee

Andrew Jackson was the first President born in a log cabin of a poor family. His father and mother had come from Ireland only two years before his birth. His father died before he was born; his mother died when he was fourteen. He had little formal education, but he learned to read. When he was nine years old he read the Declaration of Independence aloud for a group of frontiersmen who could not read. When some of these frontiersmen formed a Revolutionary Army unit, the boy watched their crude drilling. At thirteen he could no longer just watch. He joined the army himself. Already an excellent horseman, he carried messages from one unit to another. A year later he was captured by the British. One day Jackson was cut across the head when he refused to clean an English officer's boots. The blow left a scar on his face. But more than that,

for the rest of his life he hated the English and was fiercely proud of America.

After the war Jackson studied law, then moved farther west to the frontier village of Nashville, in what is now Tennessee.

Tall, handsome, and popular, Jackson liked life on the frontier. He gambled on horses, cockfights, and business. He made money and lost it and made it again. Reckless and hot-tempered, he was wounded twice in duels. Once he killed a man who he thought had insulted his wife.

When the people in Tennessee raised an army to fight the Creek Indians, Jackson was elected general. He had no military training, but he proved to be an excellent general. He defeated the Creek Indians. The next year, 1814, he was made a general in the federal army. In the last battle of the War of

Andrew Jackson, as a boy of 13, being struck by a British officer for refusing to clean the older man's boots

1812 he defeated the British at New Orleans and became a national hero.

At this time Florida still belonged to Spain. Seminole Indians living in Florida sometimes made raids across the Georgia border. President Monroe sent Jackson with a small army to stop these raids.

The hot-headed Jackson said the Spanish were protecting the Seminoles and that Florida really ought to belong to the United States. So he not only chased the Seminoles into Florida, he attacked and captured the Spanish city of Pensacola. This could have led to war with Spain—and that would have been all right with Jackson. However, Secretary of State John Quincy Adams managed to keep the peace.

In 1824 the people of Tennessee nominated Jackson for President. It may be that Jackson did not really want to be elected. He had already been elected to Congress three different times, and each time he had quit before his term was up. He was quoted as saying, "Do you think that I am such a darned fool as to think myself fit for the presidency? No sir . . . I can command a body of men in a rough way, but I am not fit to be President."

In the election Jackson was defeated by John Quincy Adams. Jackson's friends told him he had been cheated. This was not true, but Jackson believed his friends. From that day he set out to defeat Adams as he might have set out to win a battle.

By the next election in 1828 the old

Federalist party was all but dead. The Republican party, founded by Thomas Jefferson, was also breaking into groups. Of these, the more democratic group was led by Jackson. It was called the Democratic Republican party, but dropped the word *Republican* and became the Democratic party. The more conservative group was led by John Quincy Adams. It was called the National Republican party, then later changed its name to the Whig party. And so the United States had two new political parties.

At this time people from all over the United States were moving west. New states were coming into the Union and new frontiers were being opened. There was a feeling that now was the time to find new, more democratic rules of government. The old rule that only men who owned property could vote was being changed.

Jackson himself was a frontiersman. He came from a poor family. To the people moving west, looking for new land and a new life, he was a hero. In the election of 1828 Jackson was swept into office.

From all over the country the com-

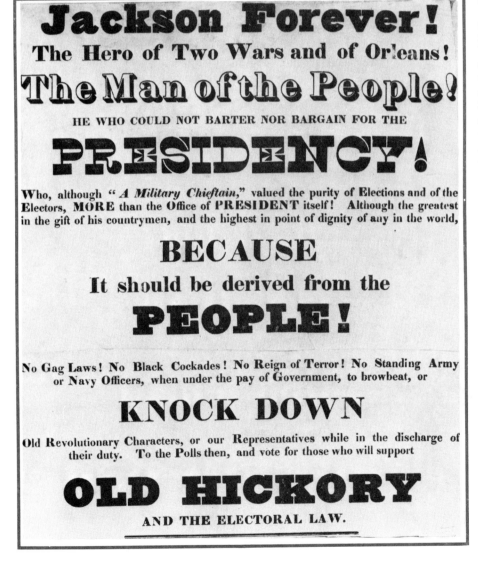

A poster from Jackson's 1828 presidential campaign. He was nicknamed Old Hickory by the troops he commanded in the War of 1812. When Jackson ate the same meager food and slept on the ground like the other soldiers, they said, "He's as tough as hickory."

mon people who admired Jackson came to hear him take the oath of office. Afterward the new President held open house. Thousands of people crowded into the White House, climbing on chairs to get a better view. Furniture was broken and fights started. Jackson escaped from the building to avoid bodily harm from his supporters. Many of the old, well-to-do families in the East thought that the rule of "King Mob" had started.

Most of the Presidents before Jackson had left lawmaking up to Congress. Jackson said it was his job to help people get the laws they wanted, and no others. Time and again he vetoed laws that Congress passed. And he urged the passage of others. People who did not like Jackson said he was trying to act like a king. They called him King Andrew the First. But most of the people, especially in the West, liked what he did. In 1832 he was elected to a second term.

In South Carolina many people did not like the Tariff Act of 1832 that had been passed by Congress. It was a law that heavily taxed goods imported from Britain and other countries. The southern states were against this tariff. The South Carolina state legislature passed its own law which said that the federal law would not be enforced in South Carolina.

Andrew Jackson believed in states'

The massive crowds that descended on the White House to celebrate Jackson's inauguration in 1829

rights, but only so far. He said no one state had the right to decide which national laws it would obey and which it would not. If this were so, the Union itself would fall apart. Jackson said he would enforce the national laws even if it meant war with South Carolina. He got ready to fight. Fortunately a compromise was worked out. But Jackson had showed, as Lincoln would later, what a strong President could do to save the Union.

From the modern point of view Jackson had many faults. He believed in slavery. He thought that the only good Indian was a dead Indian—or at least one pushed out of the white man's territory. But no President except Washington did as much to make the office of President strong. He was one of the few Presidents to finish his second term as popular as when he began his first one.

MARTIN VAN BUREN

8th President of the United States, 1837–1841

Born: December 5, 1782, in Kinderhook, New York
Died: July 24, 1862, in Kinderhook, New York

Martin Van Buren's father was a farmer and tavern keeper in Kinderhook, New York. Martin was born there. He was the first President to be born after the United States became an independent nation.

Van Buren went to school for only a few years. When he was fourteen he got a job in a lawyer's office and at twenty-one became a lawyer himself.

He was a successful lawyer. He was also interested in politics and held a number of state offices. He used these offices to give jobs to people who would vote for him and for his political friends. In this way he built up a large following. In 1821 he was elected to the U.S. Senate and was reelected in 1827.

At this time Andrew Jackson was running for President. Van Buren was a very smart politician, but he did not inspire fierce love and loyalty like Andrew Jackson. Van Buren knew this.

And he knew his own political future might depend on Jackson. So he worked hard to help Jackson win the election. When Jackson was elected he appointed Van Buren secretary of state.

Van Buren made a good secretary of state. Even so, there were other men in Jackson's Cabinet who were much more famous. No one suspected that Van Buren would ever become President.

Van Buren made a point of getting to know Jackson personally. Even though Van Buren disliked horseback riding, he rode with Jackson to win his favor. When Jackson ran for a second term, he asked that Van Buren be made Vice President. And it was largely because of Jackson's help that Van Buren was elected President in 1836.

At this point one of the worst economic depressions, or slumps, in history hit the country. One business after another failed. Banks had to close their doors. All over the country hungry men and women walked the streets without jobs.

There were many causes for this depression. It was caused in part by former policies of Andrew Jackson. Chiefly, however, the depression was caused by a wild spirit of gambling that had swept the country. Everywhere people had been buying land with borrowed money, hoping the price of the land would go up. People had borrowed money to start new businesses, then needed more money to keep them going. So it was the people themselves who were largely to blame. Nobody,

however, likes to blame himself. So the people turned on Van Buren.

Van Buren was trying hard to be a good President. Yet he was easy to blame. He was a dapper dresser and he liked to eat well. His enemies said he drank foreign wines and used gold forks and silver plates.

This was the same kind of gossip that Van Buren had once spread to help Andrew Jackson defeat John Quincy Adams. Now it was enough to make hungry people without jobs vote against Van Buren. In the election of 1840 he was defeated by William Henry Harrison.

A daguerreotype of Martin Van Buren, taken between 1845 and 1850

WILLIAM HENRY HARRISON

9th President of the United States, March to April 1841

Born: February 9, 1773, at Berkeley Plantation
in Charles City County, Virginia
Died: April 4, 1841, in Washington, D.C.

When William Henry Harrison was fourteen, he went to Hampden-Sidney College. He studied the Greek and Latin classics and liked to read them all his life. Later he studied medicine because his father wanted him to. But when his father died, Harrison quit school and joined the army. For several years he served on the northwest frontier and fought against the Indians.

Harrison was only twenty-seven when he was appointed governor of the Indiana Territory. He served in this office for twelve years. During this time the famous chief Tecumseh took a stand against further white expansion into the Northwest and the Southwest. The Indians resented being forced off their traditional hunting grounds with the promise that it would never happen again. Those promises kept being broken. In 1811 Tecumseh and his followers massed on the banks of the Tippecanoe River. General Harrison led about a thousand soldiers against them. It wasn't really a very big or important battle, but it made Harrison famous. He was given the nickname Old Tippecanoe.

During the War of 1812 Harrison served as a general in the American army. He won one of the few United States victories on the Canadian border. He served briefly in Congress. Then for several years he lived on his farm in North Bend, Ohio. He thought he had left public life forever.

However, people still remembered Old Tippecanoe.

In 1840 Martin Van Buren ran for a second term. The Whigs named only one man to run against him—Harrison.

Harrison had never taken a very large part in politics. He was much better known as a military hero than a politician. But the Whigs needed a popular hero, not a politician. They did not even say what Harrison or the Whig party believed in. They just ran against Van Buren's record as President.

At this time the country was in the middle of a very bad depression. Many people were out of jobs. The Whigs blamed this on Van Buren. They said he was rich and did not care about the people. At the same time they said nothing about Harrison's well-bred background. Instead, they talked about him as an Indian fighter. Though Harrison had grown up in a large mansion in North Bend, Ohio, there had once been a log cabin on the property. So the Whigs said their hero lived in a log cabin. They said Van Buren lived in a "palace," as they called the White House, and drank wine while Harrison drank plain hard cider. This became known as the "log cabin and hard cider campaign."

None of this had anything to do with which man would make a better President. But it was a time when Americans' heroes were frontiersmen and Indian fighters. And in 1840 Harrison was elected President.

As soon as Harrison took office long lines of people were asking him for jobs. He was a kindly man. He wanted to help and he worked hard. Worn out by his campaign, his inauguration speech (which was the longest in history— one hour and forty-five minutes), and the favor seekers, Harrison caught a cold. The cold turned into pneumonia and Harrison died one month after his inauguration. He is remembered for having the shortest term of all the Presidents.

William Harrison drinking cider in front of a simple log cabin. This image of Harrison as a poor man of the people was completely false (he owned a 2,000-acre farm) but helped elect him President.

JOHN TYLER
10th President of the United States, 1841–1845

Born: March 29, 1790, near Greenway, Virginia
Died: January 18, 1862, in Richmond, Virginia

John Tyler's father was a governor of Virginia and a friend of Thomas Jefferson's. The boy grew up believing with all his heart in states' rights. He thought that the powers of the federal government should be very limited.

He graduated from William and Mary College when he was seventeen. At twenty-one he was elected to the Virginia legislature. Later he served in the House of Representatives, as governor of Virginia, and in the U.S. Senate. But he wasn't at all well known outside his own state.

The Whig party nominated Tyler for Vice President mainly because he was from the South. Harrison was from the West, and the Whigs wanted a Vice President who could help get the southern vote. Tyler was a good-looking, courteous, soft-spoken man from a good family. He was well liked in his home state, and the Virginia vote was important. So the Whigs nominated

him. They didn't expect him ever to be President. Nobody bothered to think about what kind of President he might make.

His record in Congress showed clearly what he believed in. Like his father's friend, Thomas Jefferson, he thought the federal government should keep out of the states' business. He had always voted against spending federal money for such things as roads and harbors. He had originally been a Democrat, not a Whig, and had supported Andrew Jackson for President. But Tyler thought Jackson took too much power for the federal government. Tyler turned against him. It was largely because of this that Tyler was regarded as a Whig, although none of his ideas had changed. He still believed strongly in states' rights.

Even so, the Whigs were not really worried at first. Until this time no President had ever died in office. Many people thought that on Harrison's death Tyler did not really become President, but only "acting President" until the next election. They thought this would be a sort of caretaker's job. Also, Tyler kept in his Cabinet the same men Harrison had appointed. These were all good Whigs. They were sure Tyler would do as they told him.

It didn't take long to find out they were wrong.

Daniel Webster, the secretary of state, told Tyler that President Harrison had agreed to let a majority of his Cabinet make the important decisions. Tyler told Webster that he, as President, would make his own decisions. The Whigs wanted to start a national bank. Tyler didn't believe in national banks and vetoed the law. The Whigs rewrote it. Tyler vetoed it again.

The Whig leaders met and declared that Tyler was no longer a member of the Whig party. Every member of the Cabinet except one quit. Tyler appointed a new Cabinet.

And that is the way things went during most of the four years Tyler was President. The Whigs hated him. The Democrats didn't want him. Many politicians put party loyalty ahead of everything else. To such men Tyler was a traitor. He was known as the President without a party.

Tyler was in his fifties but looked younger. His wife died soon after he became President and he married again. His second wife, Julia Gardiner, was thirty years younger than he was. Tyler was the first President to be married while in office.

Tyler did one important thing as President. At that time Texas had broken away from Mexico and wanted to join the United States. It was legal to own slaves in Texas. And many people in the North did not want another slave state in the Union. But Tyler was from Virginia and he believed in slavery. He asked the Senate to approve a treaty taking Texas into the Union. The Senate refused.

In the election of 1844, Tyler was eager to be reelected for two reasons: He was ambitious, and he wanted to make sure Texas came into the Union. But neither the Whigs nor the Democrats wanted him. When he tried to form a third party, it failed.

The Democrats, however, did say they were in favor of Texas joining the Union. They won the election. And then Congress, without waiting for the new President to take office, passed the bill admitting Texas. Tyler signed it, one of his last acts as President.

When Tyler's term was over, he went back to Virginia. Later, as the Civil War was beginning, he was elected to the Confederate Congress. He died, however, before that Congress ever met.

JAMES POLK

11th President of the United States, 1845–1849

Born: November 2, 1795, in Mecklenburg County, North Carolina
Died: June 15, 1849, in Nashville, Tennessee

James Polk was born in North Carolina, but when he was eleven years old his family moved to Tennessee. This was still frontier country. James Polk's father was a farmer, but the boy was too sickly to do much work on the farm. He rarely took part in the rough games of other boys. Instead he spent most of his time reading. He graduated with top honors from the University of North Carolina, then studied law.

From the first, Polk was interested in politics. He was elected to the U.S. House of Representatives, and from 1835 to 1839 he was speaker of the House. Polk was a great admirer of Andrew Jackson and worked to pass the laws Jackson wanted.

Polk quit Congress to run for governor of Tennessee. He was elected, but in 1841 he was defeated for a second term. In 1843 he was defeated again. At this point it might have seemed that his career was over. He had never been

really well. He was in pain much of the time. Certainly most men would have given up. But Polk had a lonely, cold, fierce, driving spirit that would not let him quit.

In 1844, when the Democratic convention met to name a candidate for President, some people thought Martin Van Buren would be chosen. A few people thought Polk might be named for Vice President, but most people did not know much about him.

To win the nomination a candidate needed two thirds of the votes. At first Van Buren had more than half the votes, but he could not get two thirds. It began to look as if nobody could be named. Then Andrew Jackson came out for Polk. Since nobody else could win, the convention agreed on Polk as a compromise. This made him the first "dark horse" candidate for President—that is, a man who was not well known before he ran for the office. The

Whig candidate was Henry Clay, one of the most famous men in America at that time.

Texas became the big issue in the campaign. Polk and the Democratic party wanted Texas in the Union. Clay also wanted Texas, but he was sure it would cause war with Mexico. And he did not want war. So Clay never made clear just where he and the Whig party stood.

Another question in this election was who owned the Oregon Territory. Oregon was the name given to all the land between Alaska and California west of the Rocky Mountains. Both Great Britain and the United States claimed it. Now Polk and the Democrats said it must be made part of the U.S. even if it meant war.

In the 1840s many Americans were moving west. Long wagon trains streamed over the Oregon and Santa Fe Trails. A newspaper man had written that it was the "manifest destiny" of the United States to stretch from coast to coast. The phrase caught on. Everybody talked about the manifest destiny of the young nation. The country was growing and needed more room. So the people elected the "dark horse" Polk. As soon as the election was over, Congress voted to annex Texas. They didn't even wait until Polk took office.

Polk said there were still four things he wanted to do as President. They were: to lower the tariff—a tax paid on foreign goods brought into the United States; to set up a national treasury; to settle the question of the Oregon Territory; and, above all, to make California a part of the Union.

Congress quickly passed laws to set up a treasury and to lower the tariff paid on foreign goods. But for a while it looked as if there might actually be a war with England over the Oregon

Hundreds of pioneer families like this one moved west in their covered wagons.

Territory. Polk did not want to fight England. England did not want to fight either, so it was fairly easy for the two countries to reach a compromise. They agreed to run the Canadian border straight west to the Pacific, splitting the Oregon Territory between the United States and Canada. This is our present border.

That left California, the most important issue of all to Polk. Yet actually he knew very little about California. He had read that it was a lush and beautiful land. He knew it belonged to Mexico, but Mexico had only a few settlers there. What really bothered Polk was the fear that England or France might take over this land if he did not grab it first.

Polk tried to buy California. Mexico would not sell. He tried again, but it only made the Mexicans angry.

Then Polk began to use other methods. First, he tried to stir up a revolution among the few American settlers in California. But they were too few and too far away. So Polk deliberately forced Mexico into a war. He did not say the war was over California. Instead, he sent an army into Texas. Mexico still claimed to own Texas. However, Mexico did not fight so long as the American army stayed north of the Nueces River. Up to this time most people considered the Nueces as the southern border of Texas. Polk now claimed Texas went to the Rio Grande, and he sent the army there. The Mexican government was forced to fight. And this gave Polk an excuse to send warships and an army to capture California.

Polk knew the Mexican government was weak and could not hope to win a war. Even so, the war turned out to be longer and bloodier than he expected. But finally Mexico was forced to surrender. In the peace treaty the United States agreed to buy from Mexico what is now all of California and Nevada and part of Utah, Arizona, and New Mexico.

President Polk refused to run for a second term. As President he had worked hard. After four years in office he was both tired and very sick. He went back to his home in Nashville, Tennessee, and died a few months later.

Gold miners at Pine Creek, California, in 1850. Once gold was discovered at Sacramento, California, on January 24, 1848, thousands of fortune seekers like these poured into the state from all over the country. These men are shoveling gold-bearing gravel into a sluice. Water washes the sand and gravel away, leaving the gold behind.

ZACHARY TAYLOR

12th President of the United States, 1849–1850

Born: November 24, 1784, in Orange County, Virginia
Died: July 9, 1850, in Washington, D.C.

Zachary Taylor was raised in the little frontier village of Louisville, Kentucky. His father had been an officer in the Revolutionary War. All his childhood Zachary heard stories about drilling and fighting.

When he was twenty-two years old Taylor joined the army as a private. Two years later he was made lieutenant. He fought in Indian campaigns and in the War of 1812. Later he fought against Chief Black Hawk and against the Seminoles in Florida. During the Seminole War, Taylor was made general.

Texas became part of the Union in 1845. At this time most people thought the Nueces River was the southern border of Texas. But President James Polk sent General Taylor with an army across the Nueces to the Rio Grande. It was this act that brought on the Mexican War.

General Taylor was not a great general, but he was a pretty good one. In the Battle of Buena Vista he defeated a Mexican army four times as large as his. With his other victories this made him a national hero.

The Whig party wanted a hero for its presidential candidate in 1848. They had two to choose from: General Taylor and General Winfield Scott. Both were professional soldiers. Except for that, they had almost nothing in common. Scott dressed in handsome uniforms. His boots were always polished. His soldiers had nicknamed him Old Fuss and Feathers. Taylor wore the same dirty clothes he wore on his farm. His soldiers called him Old Rough and Ready.

In the young, tough frontier nation of 1848, Old Fuss and Feathers did not have a chance against Old Rough and Ready. The Whigs nominated Taylor as their candidate and he was elected.

No man ever became President knowing less about what he was supposed to do. Taylor was simply a soldier, used to giving and taking orders. He was totally honest, blunt, straightforward. And he did not know how to work with politicians.

At this time thousands of Americans were heading west. They wanted the new western territory to be made into states. But would slavery be allowed in the new states or not?

The South wanted more slave states. Most of the country did not. Some southern congressmen began to talk about leaving the Union.

Most people had expected President Taylor to favor slavery. He had been born in the South. He owned slaves on his plantation in Louisiana. But above everything else he wanted to protect the Union. He called in the southern congressmen who were talking about secession. He told them that if they tried to break up the Union, he, personally, would lead an army against them.

Slowly Congress worked out a compromise on the question of slavery in the new states. President Taylor did not like it. He might have vetoed it. But suddenly, on the Fourth of July, 1850, he became ill. Five days later he died.

MILLARD FILLMORE

13th President of the United States, 1850–1853

Born: January 7, 1800, in Locke, New York
Died: March 8, 1874, in Buffalo, New York

Millard Fillmore's father had a small farm in the Finger Lakes area of New York State. It was not much more than a clearing hacked out of the woods on the frontier. The boy worked there until he was fifteen.

Young Fillmore went to a one-room school whenever he could. This was not often. At eighteen he was a tall, good-looking boy, out of place among the seven- and eight-year-olds in the same room. The teacher was a pretty red-haired girl named Abigail Powers. She taught him so well that when he was twenty he moved to Buffalo, New York, and got a job teaching. At the same time he studied law. Before long he was admitted to the bar and married Abigail.

Fillmore quickly became a success. In 1832 he was elected to Congress as a member of the Whig party. In Congress he voted against admitting Texas to the Union, because it permitted slavery. In 1848 the Whig party nominated Zachary Taylor for President and Fillmore for Vice President. They were elected.

In his new office, Fillmore presided over one of the most important debates in American history. Would the new western territories be free states or slave states? Both of the parties, the Democrats and the Whigs, were split on the question. The senators from the South wanted slavery. Most of the senators from the North wanted the territories to be free. Some southerners began to talk about seceding from the Union.

Senator Henry Clay, from Kentucky, offered a compromise. Later it became known as the Compromise of 1850. Its main point was that California would come into the Union as a free state. In return there would be a law called the Fugitive Slave Act. By this law an owner could follow his runaway slave into a free state and recapture him, and it would be against the law to help a slave run away.

After Zachary Taylor's sudden death, Fillmore became President. President Fillmore did not like slavery. But he thought the compromise law was fair to both sides. He hoped it would settle the question of slavery and hold the Union together. Largely because of President Fillmore's influence, Congress passed the Compromise of 1850.

This compromise made many people in the North more opposed to slavery than ever.

Because Fillmore signed this law, many Whigs in the North turned against him. As a result he was not nominated by the Whig party for re-election. And before long the whole party began to fall apart. Fillmore was the last Whig President.

As President, Fillmore did do one thing of lasting importance. For two hundred years Japan had refused to trade or to have anything to do with other countries. In 1853 Fillmore sent Commodore Matthew Perry to visit Japan. Perry met with the Japanese emperor, who agreed to let American trading ships visit Japan. This became known as the "opening" of Japan.

Slaves planting sweet potatoes on a South Carolina plantation in 1862

FRANKLIN PIERCE

14th President of the United States, 1853–1857

Born: November 23, 1804, in Hillsboro, New Hampshire
Died: October 8, 1869, in Concord, New Hampshire

Franklin Pierce came from a well-known New England family. His father was twice governor of New Hampshire. During his father's second term, Franklin was elected to the state legislature. Later he was elected to the United States House of Representatives, and then to the United States Senate. He was the youngest member of the Senate.

As a young Congressman Pierce had married the pretty daughter of the president of Bowdoin College. Two of their three sons died while still very young. Mrs. Pierce was often sick. She was shy and did not like the social life in Washington. Finally she persuaded her husband to quit the Senate and go back to New Hampshire.

When the Mexican War started, Pierce enlisted as a private. President Polk promptly made him a colonel, then a general, although he had no military experience.

In 1852 a convention met in Baltimore to name the Democratic party's candidate for President. At this time Pierce was little known outside his home state. Everybody thought the candidate would be one of the leaders of the party. But none of the well-known men could get enough votes to win. Finally, on the forty-ninth ballot, Pierce was named as a compromise. But he won the election and became President.

As President, Pierce wanted to get more land for the United States. He wanted to take over Hawaii, which was still independent, but nothing came of it. He tried to buy Cuba from Spain, but only made Spain angry. But he did manage to buy a narrow strip of land from Mexico. Today this forms the southwestern corner of New Mexico and all of southern Arizona. It was called the Gadsden Purchase.

At this time a senator named Stephen Douglas wanted to build a railroad from Chicago to the Pacific. He wanted it to go through Kansas because he owned land there. Other senators wanted it built in other places. In order to get southern support for this railroad, Douglas proposed a law called the Kansas-Nebraska Act. The law would do away with the Missouri Compromise of 1820. That compromise had drawn a line across America. Slavery was declared illegal in all lands north of that line. The new Kansas-Nebraska Act would allow each territory to decide for itself whether or not to have slavery, no matter how far north it was. That was just what the southern states wanted.

Many men knew that the Kansas-Nebraska Act would cause bitter trouble between the North and South.

Somehow Pierce did not seem to understand this. So he pushed the law through Congress.

Now each territory could vote on slavery for itself. Men from the South rushed into Kansas so they could vote for slavery. Men from the North rushed in to vote against it. The fighting was so bitter that the new territory was often called Bleeding Kansas.

All over the nation people were arguing about slavery—was it right or wrong? By the end of Franklin Pierce's first term the nation was hurtling toward its most terrible tragedy, the Civil War. A new antislavery party, called the Republican party, was formed. And northerners in Pierce's own Democratic party would not nominate him for a second term. He went back home to New Hampshire. But even there he was not popular anymore.

A drawing of the armed ruffians who poured into Kansas so they could vote for or against slavery

JAMES BUCHANAN

15th President of the United States, 1857–1861

Born: April 23, 1791, near Mercersburg, Pennsylvania
Died: June 1, 1868, in Lancaster, Pennsylvania

James Buchanan's father owned a small country store in Pennsylvania near the Maryland border. The boy learned to add and subtract and keep books by clerking in the store. Later he studied law and went into politics. He was over six feet tall, broad-shouldered, and dignified. When he was twenty-three years old, he was elected to the state legislature. At thirty he was elected to Congress. He belonged to the Federalist party, but this party was slowly breaking up. Buchanan became a Democrat.

President Polk appointed Buchanan his secretary of state. He helped settle the problems of the Oregon Territory and the Mexican War. Buchanan believed the United States ought to get more and more territory. Once he wrote that the U.S. should try to buy Cuba from Spain. If Spain would not sell, Buchanan said, the U.S. should take Cuba by force.

By the election of 1856 slavery had become the biggest problem facing the United States. Many people in the North wanted to end slavery altogether, North and South. Southern slave owners wanted slavery made legal in all the territories.

The new Republican party was against slavery. Their candidate was John C. Fremont. Their slogan was "Freedom, Freemen, and Fremont."

The Democratic party did not want to take any strong stand on slavery one way or the other. They hoped this wouldn't anger anybody, either in the North or South, and would help them win votes. Nobody was quite sure just where Buchanan stood on slavery. So the Democrats made him their candidate. It was a close election, but Buchanan won.

Buchanan had been in office for only two days when the U.S. Supreme Court handed down a decision that highly

Mail was carried between Missouri and California by the Pony Express from April 1860 to October 1861, when the telegraph replaced it.

pleased the slave owners in the South. It was called the Dred Scott decision. The Supreme Court said that slavery had to be legal in all United States territories not yet made into states.

Buchanan agreed with this decision. He did not like slavery, but he thought that under the Constitution the Union had no right to stop it. He hoped that the Dred Scott decision would end the argument. Instead, it only made matters worse. When new problems arose, Buchanan sided with the South in the hope that this would keep the southern states from seceding.

By the election of 1860 slavery was the one all-important question. The Democratic party split over the question. One group favored the North, one the South. But neither group nominated Buchanan. The Republican party nominated a tall, gaunt man named Abraham Lincoln.

Lincoln won, but there was a period of several months before he took office. For Buchanan these months proved the hardest of his four years as President.

One southern state after another seceded from the Union. With all his heart Buchanan wanted to hold the Union together. But he was not sure what to do. He did not believe that any state had the right to secede. At the same time he did not believe the Union had the right to force a state to stay in the Union. Also, he was hopeful—he was always hopeful—that if he did nothing, the states that had left the Union would decide to rejoin.

And so he did nothing.

On March 4, 1861, Lincoln became President. A few weeks later the Civil War began. And at long last Buchanan made up his mind. The North, he said, must back President Lincoln "to a man," no matter what the price.

ABRAHAM LINCOLN

16th President of the United States, 1861–1865

Born: February 12, 1809, in Hardin County, Kentucky
Died: April 15, 1865, in Washington, D.C.

Abraham Lincoln's father was a ne'er-do-well farmer who drifted from one place to another along the frontier. When Abe was eight years old the family moved to Spencer County, Indiana. Abe helped to build the cabin they lived in. It had only three walls. On the open side a fire had to be kept going day and night.

Lincoln had little schooling. "There were some schools, so called," he said. But all they taught was "readin', writin', and cipherin'. . . . Of course, when I came of age I did not know much. Still, somehow, I could read. . . ." And he loved to read. There were few books on the frontier, but Lincoln borrowed all he could. At night he read by the light of an open fire.

In time Lincoln's family moved from Indiana to Illinois. By now Abe was six feet four inches tall, thin, awkward, homely looking. His coarse black hair stood up on his head. Outdoor work had made his arms and shoulders unusually strong.

Lincoln's voice was high-pitched. It sounded strange coming from such a tall, powerful body. Yet even as a boy he had a great gift for telling stories. He could make people laugh. And people liked him. He did not inspire hero worship like Andrew Jackson. He was too awkward and homely for people to think of him as a hero. But people trusted him. They believed in him.

As a young man Lincoln got a job on a flatboat going to New Orleans. Back in Illinois he got a job in a country store. The store failed and he got other odd jobs. He worked as a surveyor. Finally a friend told him he ought to be a lawyer. It was easier to be a lawyer then than it is now. Lincoln borrowed books and studied. He was always quick to learn. He became a lawyer and was elected to the state legislature. Then he was elected to Congress.

Lincoln was born in this log cabin on Rock Spring Farm, in Kentucky. It had little more than a dirt floor, a bed of wooden planks, and a window opening.

In Congress, Lincoln proposed one important law. He said the government should buy all the slaves in the District of Columbia and set them free. The law did not pass, but it showed how Lincoln felt. He believed slavery was wrong. But he did not believe slavery could be abolished without payment to the slave owners.

Lincoln did not win a second term in Congress. He went back to Illinois to practice law. For a few years he took little part in politics.

It seemed as if Lincoln's public life was over. But the question of slavery was being debated more and more throughout the country. New territory was being opened in the West; new states were coming into the Union. Should they be free or slave?

Lincoln was opposed to the spread of slavery. More than that, he wanted to help the poor of any race. He knew what it was to be poor. He began to make speeches in favor of keeping the territories free. "New free states," he said, "are places for poor people to go and better their condition." They should not be turned over to rich slave owners.

In 1858, the Illinois Republican party asked Lincoln to run for the Senate against Stephen Douglas. Douglas was in favor of letting each new state decide for itself whether or not to have slaves. In a famous series of speeches, Lincoln and Douglas debated this question. Douglas won the election. But the Lincoln-Douglas debates made Lincoln famous. It was partly because of this that the Republican party named him to run for President two years later. Lincoln was also from Illinois, a state the Republicans wanted to carry.

It was a bitter election. The Democratic party split in two, one part in the South, one in the North. A new third party tried to find some kind of compromise. Lincoln and the Republicans came out against the spread of slavery.

The election was held in the fall of 1860. Lincoln won, but he was not to take office until March 1861. In the meanwhile one southern state after another voted to leave the Union and set up a new government. President Buchanan let them go, not knowing what else to do.

On March 4, 1861, Lincoln became President. A month went by and he took no action. There were a number of reasons for this. Several of the border states had not yet decided whether to secede or stay in the Union. Lincoln wanted to hold these states if he could. Also there were a number of people in the North who did not believe either the Union or slavery was worth fighting about. Lincoln knew that if he started a war himself, many of these people would not support it. But his determination to save the Union never wavered.

On April 12, 1861, southern soldiers fired on the Union-held Fort Sumter in Charleston, South Carolina. This was the start of the War Between the States (later called the Civil War). A great wave of patriotism swept the North. Lincoln knew that now the people would support him.

The next four years were probably the most desperate in the history of the United States. In these years Lincoln proved himself to be a great Pres-

A campaign ribbon promoting Lincoln for President and Andrew Johnson for Vice President, from the campaign of 1864

ident. Even so, there was a while when he made many mistakes. He tried one general after another before he found a really good one. He did not get along too well with his own Cabinet. Some of them did not understand this tall, gaunt man who always looked as if he had bought his clothes second-hand from a man four inches shorter than he was.

Lincoln's great gift was his ability to make the common people understand and believe in what he was doing. His purpose was to save the Union because to him the Union was not just a group of states that had gotten together to form a government. It was the only important democratic government in the world. If it were destroyed, it would mean that free men

Lincoln (center) at the Union Army camp in Antietam, Maryland, in October 1862 during the Civil War. Major Pinkerton is at the left and General McClerhand at the right.

were not able to govern themselves. The fight to save the Union was the fight to save free government all over the world.

Somehow he made the people understand this. He made them understand how wrong slavery was. He made them understand that the war touched on the great principle that all people are created free and equal before God.

In the past Lincoln had not believed that under the Constitution, the federal government had the right simply to declare an end to slavery. Yet what good would it do to hold the Union together by force if slavery, which had caused the war in the first place, was not ended? Lincoln thought more and more about this as the war went on. Finally "the moment came," he said, "when I felt that slavery must die that the nation might live." And so on September 22, 1862, he issued his Emancipation Proclamation. This stated that on January 1, 1863, all slaves in any state still in rebellion against the Union would be free.

The Emancipation Proclamation did not actually free any slaves at all. It applied only to the rebellious states where Lincoln had no power to enforce it. Slavery was still legal in several of the border states that had not left the Union. Lincoln believed that to end slavery in these states, the Constitution would have to be amended. He began to work toward such an amendment. (When it did pass, it was the Thirteenth Amendment.)

Although the Emancipation Proclamation itself did not end slavery, it did make clear one important reason for the war. And it won sympathy for the North throughout the civilized world. In this way it contributed to the North's final victory.

For Lincoln the entire war was a period of much personal grief. He was always aware of the death and suffering on both sides. Men saw him walking the streets at night, alone, deep in thought. Sometimes in rain or fog he wore a shawl around his shoulders, his long neck bent forward, the lines of his bony face drawn deep with sorrow.

By the fall of 1864 it was clear the North was winning the war. Lincoln was easily elected to a second term.

Lincoln never wanted revenge upon the South. Instead he said, "Blood cannot restore blood, and government should not act for revenge." He only wanted to restore the Union, as quickly and peacefully as possible. In his second inaugural address he told how he believed the nation should act:

"With malice toward none, with charity for all, with firmness in the right, as God gives us to see the right, let us strive on to finish the work we are in, to bind up the nation's wounds, to care for him who shall have borne the battle, and for his widow and his orphan—to do all which may achieve and cherish a just and lasting peace among ourselves and with all nations."

This was his dream. It was not to be.

On April 9, 1865, General Robert E. Lee surrendered to Lincoln's general, U.S. Grant, in a house in the small village of Appomattox Courthouse, Virginia. On the night of April 14, five days later, President and Mrs. Lincoln went to see a play at a Washington theater. During the play an actor named John Wilkes Booth stepped into the box behind Lincoln and shot him in the back of the head. The next day one of the greatest men in all American history lay dead.

It is probable that Booth, in some crazed way, believed he was helping the South. But, in fact, Lincoln's death hurt the South a great deal. Had Lincoln lived, he might have brought the South back into the Union with the least possible bloodshed and bitterness. Without Lincoln some of the worst men, both North and South, came into power.

The assassination of Lincoln at Ford's Theater in Washington, D.C. From left to right: Major Rathbone, Miss Harris, First Lady Mary Lincoln, the President, and John Wilkes Booth.

ANDREW JOHNSON

17th President of the United States, 1865–1869

Born: December 29, 1808, in Raleigh, North Carolina
Died: July 31, 1875, in Carter Station, Tennessee

Andrew Johnson's father worked as a sort of handyman in a tavern in Raleigh, North Carolina. His mother was a maid in the same tavern. Johnson's father died when the boy was three years old and his mother had to take in washing to help feed her children. Young Andy never went to school. As a young boy he was apprenticed to a tailor. Perhaps that was when he learned to read. But he hated his master. When he was sixteen he ran away to the little town of Greenville, Tennessee, and went into business for himself.

He was a good tailor and he began to make money. When he was eighteen he married Eliza McCardle. She was only sixteen, but she had been to school. She taught her husband to write and helped him with his reading.

Johnson was a stocky young man with a hard mouth and no humor in his eyes. He rarely laughed, but he had

a great drive to get ahead in the world. He began to walk several miles back and forth to a school that let him take part in student debates. He had a big, booming voice, a mind like a steel trap, and a tongue like a whip. Many of the students, far better educated than Johnson, were afraid to debate with him.

Although he had little humor, Johnson was a loving son and had a deep sense of duty. As soon as he had made a little money he brought his mother and his brothers and sisters to live with him. He always thought of himself as the champion of the poor and the weak against the rich and the strong.

Most of the people who lived in Johnson's part of Tennessee were farmers or small businessmen. They elected him to the town council before he was twenty-one. Then they elected him mayor. He was only thirty-three when elected to Congress. At forty-five he was governor of Tennessee. He served two terms and was elected to the U.S. Senate.

Andrew Johnson's father had never owned slaves. In fact, he had never owned anything. But Johnson believed that the right to own slaves was guaranteed by the Constitution. Also, he was a Democrat. In the Senate he voted with the South on almost every issue.

After Lincoln was elected, the southern states left the Union, Tennessee with them. As the states seceded, every southerner left Congress—except one. Andrew Johnson. "I voted against Lincoln," Johnson said, "I spoke against him. I spent my money to defeat him. But still I love my country."

Johnson became something of a hero in the North. And in the election of 1864 the Republicans wanted to be a "Union" party, not one representing only part of the country. So when Lincoln ran for a second term, the Republicans nominated Johnson for Vice President. They never expected him to be President. But Lincoln was murdered, and so Johnson did become President.

Johnson, like Lincoln, did not want to take revenge on the southern states. He wanted them brought back into the Union as quickly and easily as possible. Although some of the former leaders of the Confederacy were not pardoned, he gave a pardon to all southerners who would promise loyalty to the Union.

That had been Lincoln's plan. But in the United States Congress there were a number of men, called Radical Republicans, who were opposed to it. They believed the South had to be punished for having left the Union. They refused to admit the newly elected southerners to Congress.

Certainly the South was partly to blame for the trouble that followed. Although slavery had been abolished, laws were passed that said no black person could vote or sit on a jury. In some states no blacks could have a business of their own. Blacks could be arrested and forced to work for white men. In some places they were not even allowed to walk into a town without permission from a white man.

Cruel laws of this kind did not help Johnson in his efforts to help the South. Instead they made more and more people in the North agree with the Radical Republicans. More Radical Republicans were elected to Congress.

Congress began to discuss the Fourteenth and Fifteenth Amendments to the Constitution. These amendments made citizens of the former slaves and guaranteed the men among them the right to vote. Next Congress divided the South into five military districts. The federal army was sent in to take command. Southern officials were thrown out of office and new elections were held under military control.

In these elections blacks were allowed to vote, but many white southerners were not. Also the old leaders of the South were not allowed to run for office. As a result, some poor whites and former slaves who could neither read nor write were elected. They knew nothing about running a government and the state governments fell apart.

There were a number of reasons why the Radical Republicans passed these extreme laws. Some Congressmen honestly wanted to help the blacks. Some of them simply wanted to punish the South. But many of them voted for purely political reasons. Most white southerners had been Democrats. The

Black men were granted the right to vote by the Fifteenth Amendment (ratified in 1870). Women did not receive that right until 1920.

Radical Republicans even wanted the Constitution changed to make sure the Republican party would always be in power.

In the South the white people now had almost no lawful way to protect themselves. As a result, some began to use unlawful ways. Groups such as the Ku Klux Klan tried to force blacks back into the old way of life by frightening them. If fear was not enough, the Klansmen sometimes killed. They attacked northern whites who had come into the South. Some of these, called Carpetbaggers, were there only to try to make money from an unhappy situation. But the Klan also attacked and sometimes murdered good men who had come south to teach the former slaves.

Johnson did not have Lincoln's great power to persuade and lead the people. He made speeches asking for moderate treatment of the South. But his own speeches were not moderate. In fact, they were so violent that he lost voters rather than gained them.

Finally Congress decided to impeach, or get rid of, President Johnson—the first time in the history of the United States that this had happened. There were no lawful grounds for the charges brought against Johnson. They were based on anger rather than reason. But it was a time when anger, not reason, ruled much of the nation.

During the trial one of the lawyers defending Johnson told Congress: "He is a man of few ideas, but they are right and true, and he can suffer death sooner than yield up or violate one of them." It was a good picture of the President. Even so, out of fifty-four senators, thirty-six voted to impeach Johnson, and nineteen to acquit him. However,

An actual carpetbag—a suitcase made out of carpet material. Carpetbags were carried by northerners who moved into the southern states after the Civil War.

the law required a two-thirds majority to impeach. So Andrew Johnson missed being put out of office by one vote.

While this unrest was going on in the capital and in the South, trouble was also brewing in the West. Starting with Johnson's first year in office and continuing until 1886, there was almost continuous conflict between Indians and whites. Men who had fought against one another during the Civil War combined forces to fight the Indians westward across the Great Plains. They wanted to take control of the lands west of the Mississippi River so that homesteaders could settle there. The Indians fought back, trying in vain to hold on to their hunting ground. The railroads cut in half the vast buffalo herds that they depended on for food, clothing, fuel, and shelter. These animals were killed in great numbers by white "sportsmen" until the buffalo became almost extinct. Once the herds were wiped out, the Indians had the grim choice of starving or being confined in reservations.

Johnson's term ended soon after his impeachment hearing. He went back to Tennessee. And six years later he was once more elected to the U.S. Senate. Meanwhile some of the senators who had once voted against him had come to admire his courage. They stood and clapped for him when he entered the Senate.

It may have been a proud moment for the old fighter. But maybe not. He himself had not changed. He made a speech in which he defended what he had done as President and lashed out at those who had opposed him.

It was his last big speech. A short time afterward he became sick and died.

To be impeached, a President must first be tried before the U.S. Senate. Then, if two thirds of the senators agree, he can be removed from office. This drawing illustrates the voting, or the second part, of Johnson's impeachment hearings on May 16, 1868.

ULYSSES S. GRANT

18th President of the United States, 1869–1877

Born: April 27, 1822, in Point Pleasant, Ohio
Died: July 23, 1885, in Mount McGregor, New York

When he was thirty-nine years old Ulysses S. Grant was clerking in a small town store for fifty dollars a month. Before this he had quit or been fired from every job he ever had. He drank too much. Most people thought of him as a bum.

Three years later, in 1864, Grant was a lieutenant general in command of all the U.S. armies. In 1868 he was elected President of the United States. He served two terms, and seven years after he left office he was flat broke once more.

It is the strangest, most up-and-down career of any American President.

To begin with, his name wasn't even U.S. Grant. When he was seventeen years old, his father, who owned a tannery and farm near Point Pleasant, Ohio, managed to send him to West Point.

The congressman who appointed him to the military academy thought his first two names were Ulysses Simpson. (Simpson was his mother's maiden name. His real names were Hiram Ulysses.) So U.S. Grant was the name under which he was registered at West Point. And the name stuck.

As a young lieutenant, Grant served under General Zachary Taylor in the Mexican War. He admired General Taylor's coolness in battle and the sloppy way he dressed. Later, as a commanding general, Grant would be just as cool and almost as sloppy as the man he admired.

Grant was married shortly after the Mexican War. But when he was ordered to duty in the West, he could not take his family with him. He began to drink. Finally his commanding officer told him he must either quit drinking or resign. Grant resigned.

Back home, his wife's father gave him a small farm near St. Louis. Grant liked to farm. But the land was poor

Lieutenant General Grant in August 1864 during the Civil War

and he couldn't make a living. He moved to St. Louis, got a job in real estate, and failed at that. He got another job and was fired. Finally his brothers gave him a job in a store they owned in Galena, Illinois. His salary was fifty dollars a month. His family and his friends considered him a failure.

When the Civil War began in 1861, the North desperately needed trained officers. Grant was appointed a colonel in the army and rose to be a general. In March 1864, President Lincoln put him in command of all northern armies.

Grant turned out to be a great mil-

itary leader. He had a kind of bulldog quality. He saw clearly what he wanted and went for it, and kept on until he got it. The Union armies had more men and more equipment than the Confederates, and Grant used these advantages like a hammer. Men who did not like Grant called him the Butcher because of the heavy losses his forces took. But he won victories. Several times congressmen asked Lincoln to fire Grant. "I can't spare this man," Lincoln told them. "He fights."

Grant's victories brought an end to the Civil War and made him a national hero. The Republicans nominated him for President in 1868. He had never been interested in politics. He had only voted for President once in his life. But he was elected easily.

The big problem facing the nation was the reconstruction of the South. As a general, Grant had given the southern army very generous terms of surrender. But as President he left the South to Congress. And Congress, under the control of men called Radical Republicans, passed one harsh law after another against the South. When necessary, Grant ordered troops to enforce these laws.

Certainly Grant wanted to be a good President. He settled a quarrel with Great Britain that had started during the Civil War. He helped set up Yellowstone National Park, the first national park in the country. But often he seemed to know very little of what was going on around him.

Outside the army Grant proved to be a very poor judge of men. Many of those he appointed to office turned out to be crooks and thieves. Completely honest himself, he could not see what was happening. And even when he was told, he would not believe it.

By the end of his first term there were a number of people in his own party who thought Grant should not be reelected. However, they could not agree on another candidate. Grant himself was still popular with the nation. And the happy crooks in his party wanted to keep him. He was reelected by a large majority.

The scandals continued. Laws passed by Congress and enforced by federal troops established crooked state governments in the South. In the North, railroads and whiskey manufacturers bribed government officials. Other officials used political jobs to make dishonest money from the Post Office and from government business. Many of these officials had been appointed by Grant. Often they were his personal friends.

Still, everyone knew Grant himself was honest. When his second term ended he was still popular. He made a round-the-world tour. He was met with honors wherever he went. He came home and bought a large house in New York City.

Now he needed more money and he invested everything he had in a banking business. Then he left the management of the business up to "friends." He still trusted his friends. But these friends were like some he had appointed to political office. The business went bankrupt. Suddenly Grant was not only without money, but deeply in debt.

About this same time Grant, who had always been a heavy smoker, learned that he had cancer of the throat.

Grant could have lived out his time on charity. He did not want that. He wanted to pay off his debts and leave something for his family. A publisher offered him money if he would write the story of his life. Grant went to work although he knew he was dying. He was in pain much of the time. But courage was one thing the old soldier always had in plenty. Four days before his death he finished the autobiography. It not only made a fortune for his family, it turned out to be a very good and honest book.

RUTHERFORD B. HAYES

19th President of the United States, 1877–1881

Born: October 4, 1822, in Delaware, Ohio
Died: January 17, 1893, in Fremont, Ohio

Rutherford Hayes's father owned a store in Delaware, Ohio. Rutherford was a serious, hard-working boy. In elementary school he was the champion speller. Later he graduated at the top of his class from Kenyon College, then went to Harvard Law School.

When Hayes first opened his law office in Cincinnati, he had very few clients. To save money he slept in his office. But not for long. He won several big cases, and soon he had all the work he could handle.

When the Civil War began, Hayes was appointed a captain of volunteers. He had no military training, but he proved to be a very dashing officer. He was wounded four times and had four horses killed under him. Before the war was over he was a major general.

Hayes was still in the army when the Republican party asked him to run for Congress. He refused to go home and campaign. Any officer who left his post to run for political office, Hayes said, "ought to be scalped." He was elected anyway, but stayed with the army until the war was over.

Hayes served two terms in Congress, then was elected governor of Ohio. As governor he helped get blacks the right to vote. He helped start Ohio State University. He worked hard to improve the Ohio civil service—all state government employees who had nonmilitary jobs and were appointed rather than elected—and to make the state government more honest. In fact, he ran such a strict government that some of the unhappy politicians in his own party began to call him Old Granny.

As the presidential election of 1876 drew near, most persons thought the Democrats were sure to win. The Republican administration under Grant was in disgrace. The party itself was divided. Some hoped they could keep on just as they were. Others thought the only chance to win was to have a candidate known for his honesty. This group nominated Rutherford B. Hayes.

The Democratic candidate was named Samuel J. Tilden. When the election was over, Tilden had 4,284,020 votes. Hayes had 4,036,572 votes. These were popular votes—the votes of individual people all over the country. But it was the electoral college that cast the final vote. To win, 185 electoral votes were needed. Tilden had 184. Hayes had 165. But the votes of four states (20 votes in all) were contested or disputed. Both the Democrats and Republicans claimed them. Three of these states—Florida, South Carolina, and Louisiana—were in the South. Although the Civil War had been over for eleven years, there was still a great deal of argument over who could vote and who couldn't. Both the Democrats and the Republicans claimed to have won.

If Tilden got one single vote from any of these states, he would win the election. But Hayes had to get every vote to win.

In Congress the argument went on for months. The time for the new President to take office came closer and closer. And still nobody knew who the new President would be.

Finally a deal was made. The Democrats agreed to accept a decision made by a committee. The committee was to have eight Republicans and seven Democrats. Quite naturally, the committee voted eight to seven to give all the votes from all the contested states to the Republicans. This made Hayes President.

In return the Republicans promised that federal troops would be withdrawn from the South.

Hayes kept the promise. On April 24, 1877, the last federal troops left Louisiana. The long bloody period known as the Reconstruction Era was over.

But the age of immigration was just beginning. Between 1870 and 1900 more than eleven million immigrants

A collapsible lantern advertising Hayes for President, from the 1876 campaign

European immigrants waiting to be admitted to the United States at Ellis Island, New York City. Many carried all their possessions in one trunk or cardboard box.

poured into the United States from all parts of Europe and China. They came seeking work and a new life for their families. Their vast numbers helped change the United States from an agricultural to an industrial nation. They crowded into cities, competing for housing and jobs with more established Americans. Factory owners took advantage of this vast increase in cheap labor to lower wages and lengthen working hours. This paved the way for the strikes and the rise of labor unions in the 1880s.

Hayes tried hard to run an honest administration. He appointed honest men to office. He tried to get rid of some of the crooks. He ordered that no government employee should take part in politics.

Many of the professional politicians in Hayes's own party did not like some of the reforms he tried to make. Congress would not pass some of the laws he wanted for honest government. Some laws that he did not want were passed by Congress over his veto.

Because of Congress, Hayes did not make all the reforms he would have liked. But on the whole he left the federal government more honest than he found it. He refused to run for a second term and went back to his home in Ohio. He died there on January 17, 1893.

JAMES A. GARFIELD

20th President of the United States, 1881

Born: November 19, 1831, in Orange, Ohio
Died: September 19, 1881, in Elberon, New Jersey

James Garfield's father was a farmer in Cuyahoga County, Ohio. He died before James was two years old, and the child was raised by his mother and older brother. They were very poor and James had little chance to go to school.

But Garfield decided that he wanted an education. He began to go to school wherever and whenever he could. He worked at any kind of odd job that would leave him time for his books. He learned rapidly. Soon one of his favorite tricks was to write Latin with one hand and Greek with the other at the same time. Before Garfield was thirty years old, he was president of a small college.

By this time the whole nation was becoming more and more worried about the problem of slavery. Garfield believed slavery was immoral. He began to make speeches against letting the western territories become slave states.

When the Civil War began, Garfield raised a regiment of volunteer soldiers. Many of the young men had been his students.

Garfield had no military training, but he knew how to learn. He studied everything he could find on military tactics. He became an excellent officer. When he was thirty-one he was made the youngest brigadier general in the army.

Garfield was also elected to Congress from Ohio. At first he refused to leave the army. Finally President Lincoln talked him into quitting the army and taking his seat in Congress.

For the next eighteen years Garfield served in Congress. During much of this time the American people did not demand very honest government from their representatives in Congress. As a result, they did not get very honest government. Many politicians came to believe the purpose of government was

A hand-painted banner urging voters to choose Garfield for President and Chester Arthur for Vice President in 1880

to make the politicians and their friends rich. This was especially true during the administration of President Grant.

As a congressman, Garfield was accused of taking bribes. He denied the charges, and they were never proved.

In 1880 there were three well-known men in the Republican party who were trying to get the presidential nomination. But at the nominating convention none of them could get a major-ity. Finally the delegates nominated Garfield as a compromise.

During the campaign the Democrats talked a lot about the bribes Garfield was said to have taken in Congress. But they could not prove anything and Garfield won an easy victory.

Garfield began his term by fighting some of the powerful congressmen who wanted to run the government their way. Garfield said he was going to prove that the President was not just a clerk for Congress.

The federal government had almost no civil service (appointed government employees who were permanent and did not change with each new President). Several Presidents had asked Congress for good civil service laws, but Congress would not pass them. With every new administration many government workers got fired and new ones, who had voted for the administration, got hired. Each new President had to spend much of his time handing out jobs.

President Garfield did this too. Then on July 2, 1881, he was shot by a man whom he had denied a job.

The entire nation was shocked. As a result of the President's murder, people began to demand more honest government. They demanded better civil service laws that would keep honest government workers on the job. And because the people demanded it, Congress finally did improve the civil service laws.

CHESTER A. ARTHUR

21st President of the United States, 1881–1885

Born: October 5, 1829, in Fairfield, Vermont
Died: November 18, 1886, in New York, New York

Chester Arthur's career shows that sometimes the office of President may work a small miracle in the man who holds it.

As a young man, Arthur taught school, then became a lawyer. He was interested in politics, but he did not run for office himself. Instead he worked with political "bosses." These were men who tried to control elections by giving jobs and money to people who would vote the way the bosses wanted. In time Arthur became an important political boss himself.

After the Civil War, President Grant appointed Arthur the collector of the Port of New York. This was a very important political position. Arthur used it to give jobs to people who would vote and work for the Republican party. Then people had to give back part of their pay to the Republican party. They also had to vote the way they were told.

Arthur was not the only person doing this kind of thing. In fact, it was a common practice under Grant. Arthur himself did not believe it was wrong. He was a friendly, good-humored man, always very polite. People called him the Gentleman Boss.

After Grant's second term, Rutherford B. Hayes became President. Hayes said that men who held important government jobs should not take part in the management of political parties. Arthur refused to obey. He seemed to believe that his first duty was to his party, not to his country. As a result, Hayes forced him out of his job.

In 1880 the Republican party was split into two groups. One group, called the Stalwarts, wanted to nominate Ulysses S. Grant for a third term as President. The other group wanted a candidate who would insist on reform and more honest government.

Arthur was a Stalwart. He worked hard to have Grant nominated. Fi-

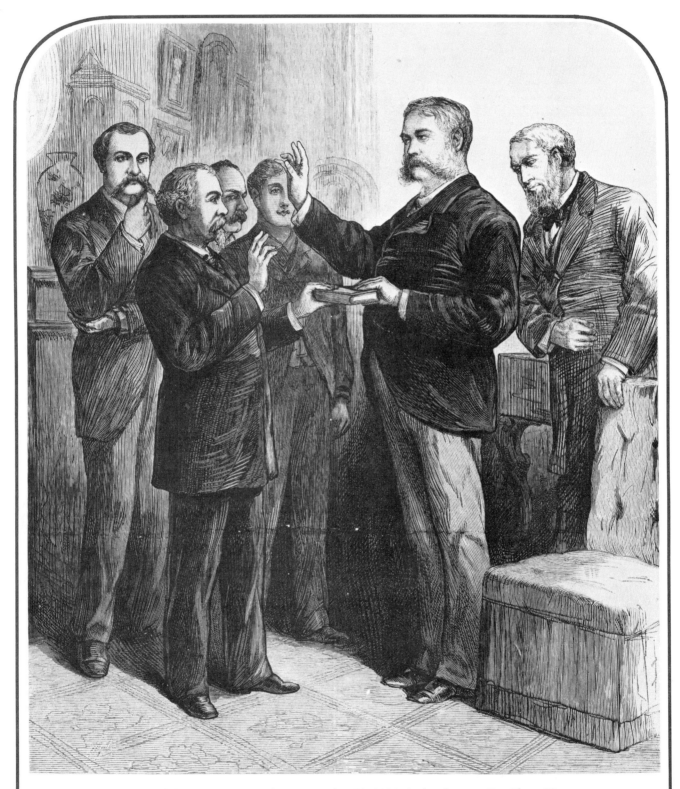

When Garfield was assassinated on September 20, 1881, Arthur became President. Here Arthur is being sworn in by Judge Brady at Arthur's home in New York City.

nally, however, James Garfield won the nomination. As a compromise, Arthur himself was nominated for Vice President. He and Garfield won the election.

As President, Garfield wanted to reform the civil service. He thought people should have to take a written examination in order to get a government job. Then the jobs would go to those who were best qualified, not just to those who voted for this or that political party. Vice President Arthur was openly opposed. He wanted things left as they were.

Garfield had been in office only a few months when he was murdered by a man named Charles Guiteau. When he shot the President, Guiteau shouted, "I am a Stalwart! Arthur is now President!" Later Guiteau said he had killed the President because Garfield had refused to give him a job.

The entire nation was shocked at the President's murder, and at the reason for it. Many people were frightened. They wondered what Arthur would be like as President. Some Stalwart politicians were happy to have Arthur become President. They thought things would go back to the way they had been under President Grant.

Everybody was in for a surprise.

Arthur could not forget that Garfield had been murdered by a man who shouted, "Arthur is now President!" He could not forget that it was the kind of politics he and other Stalwarts had stood for that had caused such a thing to happen. A change came over Arthur. He realized that as President, his duty was to all the people, not just to one party. The very size of his job made him feel humble. He tried to carry on Garfield's work and asked Congress for a new civil service law.

The old Stalwart politicians became angry at Arthur. But now the people themselves were demanding reform. In the next congressional election many of the old politicians were defeated. After that it did not take long to get the new law passed.

Arthur went on to work hard and honestly at being President. He helped bring the navy up to date with modern ships. He changed the postal system to give better and cheaper service. But the Stalwart politicians did not forgive him. They refused to nominate him for President in 1884.

Arthur went back to his home in New York. He could not be elected President on his own. But the people of the country admired him far more than they had a few years before.

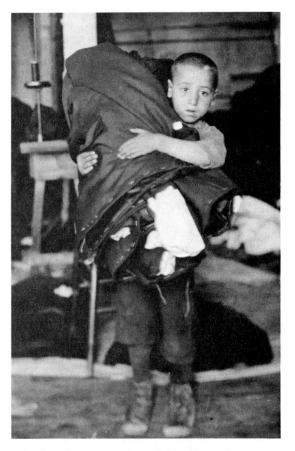

The first laws to regulate child labor and improve working conditions were passed in the 1880s.

GROVER CLEVELAND

22nd President of the United States, 1885–1889
24th President of the United States, 1893–1897

Born: March 18, 1837, in Caldwell, New Jersey
Died: June 24, 1908, in Princeton, New Jersey

Grover Cleveland's father was a Presbyterian minister with a big family and little money. When Grover was fourteen he had to quit school to work in a store. At seventeen he left home to look for a better job. He planned to go to Cleveland, Ohio, because he liked the name. On the way he stopped to visit an uncle in Buffalo, New York. There he got a job in a lawyer's office making four dollars a week. But he also had a chance to study. By the time he was twenty-two, he was a lawyer.

By then Cleveland's father had died. His mother was poor. When the Civil War started in 1861, Grover and his two brothers drew lots. Two of them would join the army, they decided; the other brother would stay at home to support their mother. Grover drew the short straw and kept working. Later his political enemies would say he stayed out of the army because he was afraid. But no one who really knew Grover Cleveland ever believed it.

Cleveland became a very successful lawyer. In 1881 he was asked by the Democratic party to run for mayor of Buffalo. Most of the people there were Republicans, but many of them were unhappy with how the city was run. They wanted a change and a more honest government.

Cleveland was elected. He gave the people an even more honest government than some of them wanted. He reorganized the city so that it ran more cheaply. He fired anybody he caught taking graft. Within a year he had cleaned up the city. Because Cleveland had such a fine record of cleaning up corruption and saving the taxpayers' money, the Democrats nominated him for governor. Running on his reputation as an honest politician, Cleveland was swept into office without making a single campaign speech.

As governor, Cleveland made sure the state got its money's worth for every dollar spent. Some of the politicians did not like it, but the people did.

In 1884 Cleveland was nominated by the Democrats to run for President. No Democrat had been elected President since the Civil War. However, at this time the Republican party was split into two groups. One group, called Mugwumps, were demanding reform and a more honest government. Because they did not like the Republican candidate, they voted for Cleveland. It was a very close election, but Cleveland won.

Cleveland began to reform the federal government as he had the state government of New York. He im-

proved the civil service to get better government workers. He forced the railroads to return eighty-one million acres of government land they had taken illegally. He made sure the navy got the best ships possible for the least money.

No President has ever worked harder than Cleveland. Often he was at his desk until two or three o'clock in the morning. He studied every bill Congress passed and vetoed more than four hundred of them. Many of these gave pensions to Civil War veterans whether or not they had been wounded. Cleveland believed this was dishonest. When one politician told him that his actions might keep him from being reelected he said, "What's the use of being elected or reelected unless

A campaign banner for Grover Cleveland

you stand for something?"

One of the big problems facing the country in 1888 was the tariff. This is a tax paid on products brought into the United States from other countries. The higher the tariff, the higher the price of these imported products. American manufacturers and workers wanted a high tariff. This allowed American manufacturers to sell their own products at a high price too. Farmers and other people wanted a low tariff so they could buy goods cheaply.

In the election of 1888 Cleveland and the Democratic party stood for a low tariff. It was a very close election. Cleveland got more popular votes than Harrison. But Harrison won in the electoral college and became President.

When Mrs. Cleveland moved out of the White House, she told the servants to take good care of it. "I want everything just the way it is now when we come back," she said. "That will be exactly four years from now."

She was right. In 1892 Cleveland and Harrison once more ran against each other. This time Cleveland won. He was the only President in U.S. history to serve two terms that did not directly follow each other.

Cleveland's second term was much like his first. He worked hard. He did what he thought was right, whether it was popular or not. When a railroad strike in Chicago interfered with the mail, Cleveland sent federal troops. He broke up the strike. "If it takes the entire army and navy to deliver one postcard in Chicago," he said, "that card will be delivered."

A serious depression swept the country. Cleveland tried to improve the treasury system rather than help the people who were out of work. His methods were not very successful. But he thought it would not be constitutional for the federal government to help individual people or businesses.

Cleveland's second term ended in 1897. And when he left office, the federal government was a better-working and more honest organization. His last words before he died were: "I have tried so hard to do right."

BENJAMIN HARRISON

23rd President of the United States, 1889–1893

Born: August 20, 1833, near North Bend, Ohio
Died: March 13, 1901, in Indianapolis, Indiana

As a boy Benjamin Harrison spent most of his time on a farm owned by his father. He always liked to read. He was a good student. By the time he was twenty-one years old, he had graduated from college and married. He moved to Indianapolis, Indiana, with his bride and became a successful lawyer there.

When the Civil War began, Harrison formed a regiment of volunteers. He was appointed colonel. His regiment took part in many battles, and Harrison proved to be a brave and good officer. After the war he went back to Indianapolis to practice law.

In January 1881 Harrison was elected to the U.S. Senate. Because his father had been a congressman and his grandfather, William Henry Harrison, had been President, Harrison's name was already well known throughout the country. It was partly for this reason that in 1888 the Republicans nomi-

nated him for President.

Harrison was a small man, only five feet six inches tall. During the Civil War his soldiers had affectionately called him Little Ben. Now the Democrats used the name to imply that he was not "big" enough to be President. In turn, the Republicans sang a song called "Grandfather's Hat Fits Ben." Cartoonists drew pictures of him as a very little man almost hidden under a huge, high-topped hat.

Harrison could think about only one subject at a time. Sometimes, deep in thought, he would walk right past people he knew without recognizing them. Because of this some people said he was cold and unfriendly. Actually he was a warm, kind-hearted man. But he was not a good "back slapping" politician. He did not like to meet big crowds of strangers. So he ran what was called a "front porch" campaign. He stayed at home and talked with

"Little Ben" Harrison, wearing his grandfather's hat

man named Theodore Roosevelt as commissioner. But not even Roosevelt could do much, because Congress did not want reform. Within one year thirty thousand postmasters were fired so that new ones, who had friends in Congress, could be appointed.

Harrison was in favor of a high tariff. With his help Congress passed the McKinley Tariff Act. This put a high tax on goods shipped to the United States from other countries. As a result, prices went up. Farmers and small businessmen complained. At the same time some of the big manufacturers were having labor troubles. Labor unions said that the power of the government was being used to help the rich and hurt the poor. Laborers organized strikes to protest working long hours for low pay in airless factories that later became known as sweatshops. They wanted children to be protected from having to do adult labor, and they demanded safe working conditions. Many of the members of the newly formed labor unions were recent immigrants. And, as time passed, more and more of these immigrants got the vote. Many voters turned against Harrison and he was defeated for reelection in 1892.

Harrison went back to his home in Indianapolis. He wrote books about United States government and continued to practice law until his death in 1901.

small groups of politicians who came to see him.

It was a very close race for President. Actually Grover Cleveland, the Democrat, got more popular votes than Harrison. But in the electoral college Harrison won 233 to 168.

As President, Harrison wanted to continue the reform of the civil service started by Cleveland. He appointed a vigorous, hard-working young

WILLIAM McKINLEY

25th President of the United States, 1897–1901

Born: January 29, 1843, in Niles, Ohio
Died: September 14, 1901, in Buffalo, New York

William McKinley was born in Niles, Ohio, a town with a population of about three hundred. When he was nine years old the family moved to Poland, Ohio, which wasn't much bigger. McKinley went to local schools, then to Allegheny College. He had been in college only a short time when he became sick and had to go home.

The Civil War had just begun. McKinley joined the army as a private. He was the first person to volunteer from his hometown. Before the war was over he was promoted to major.

After the war McKinley studied law. He began to practice in Canton, Ohio, and married Ida Saxton, the daughter of the local banker. McKinley was a pale, dignified, pleasant man. And very smart. He knew from the first what he wanted and he aimed for it. Later he told friends, "I have never been in doubt since I was old enough to think intelligently that I would some-

day be made President."

He started by running for Congress. He served there for fourteen years and became one of the leaders of the Republican party. In 1891 he was elected governor of Ohio. He made a national reputation as a businesslike executive. Then in 1896 he was nominated for President.

Like Benjamin Harrison, McKinley ran what was called a "front porch" campaign. He did this because his wife was an invalid and he was devoted to her. He refused to leave her to travel around the country for long periods of time. So the wealthy men who were backing McKinley brought people from all over the country to see him. McKinley stood on his front porch and talked to them.

The Democrats claimed McKinley would take orders from the rich bankers in the big cities. But he won the election by a large majority.

Colonel Theodore Roosevelt leads the Rough Riders in a charge to capture San Juan Hill, Cuba, during the Spanish-American War.

At this time Cuba still belonged to Spain. For several years the Cubans had been fighting for their independence. Many people in the United States wanted to help them. Some newspapers were particularly eager for the U.S. to declare war on Spain. They printed stories about how the Spanish mistreated the Cubans. These newspapers were later called the yellow press. Not all of these stories were true, but they made people angry.

McKinley did not want war. He knew that Spain had finally agreed to give Cuba its independence without fighting. But he gave in to the newspapers and on April 11, 1898, asked Congress for war with Spain.

At that time Acting Secretary of the Navy Theodore Roosevelt was keeping his eye on Spanish activity in the Pacific Ocean. Soon after McKinley asked Congress to declare war on Spain for its policies in Cuba, Roosevelt took it upon himself to send ships to the Philippine Islands. These were Spanish-owned islands in the Pacific. The American fleet soon destroyed the Spanish fleet there. So the war in the Pacific was soon over. But it took several months for the War Department to collect enough American soldiers to send to Cuba. One hundred days after McKinley's declaration of war, the United States defeated Spain in Cuba. Cuba was declared independent and the United States took control of the Philippines as well as the islands of Guam (in the Pacific) and Puerto Rico (in the Caribbean).

Even before this war with Spain there were people who wanted the United States to take over the Hawaiian Islands. Americans living in the islands had staged a revolution and overthrown the old Hawaiian government.

They wanted to become part of the United States so that they could sell sugar grown in the islands for a high price. President Cleveland had refused to recognize the new Hawaiian government. He said it had been forced on the people against their will. McKinley was not as particular. At his request Congress quickly voted to annex the islands. On July 7, 1898, Hawaii became an American territory.

In 1900 McKinley was elected to a second term. All over the country business was good. In 1901 Buffalo, New York, put on a big fair. McKinley visited it on September 6. He was in one of the buildings shaking hands with a huge crowd of people. He had just taken the flower he was wearing on his coat and had given it to a little girl when a man stepped up as if to shake hands. He had a handkerchief wrapped around his right hand. Inside the handkerchief was a gun. He fired two shots into the President. The man's name was Leon Czolgosz. He said he was an anarchist, someone who did not believe in government. He also said he wanted to kill a great ruler.

Even as McKinley lay wounded, he thought of his invalid wife. He whispered to a friend beside him, "Be careful how you tell her. Oh, be careful how you tell her."

Eight days later he died.

THEODORE ROOSEVELT

26th President of the United States, 1901–1909

Born: October 27, 1858, in New York, New York
Died: January 6, 1919, at Sagamore Hill, Long Island, New York

When he was a child, Theodore Roosevelt was sick much of the time from asthma. He decided to build up his body. He exercised endlessly—he ran and swam and lifted weights. Slowly he overcame his asthma. He developed a deep chest, powerful arms and shoulders, and great endurance.

As a boy Roosevelt never went to a regular school. Because of his poor health, he had private tutors. At eighteen he entered Harvard University. He got fair grades, graduated at twenty-two, and was married the same year.

Roosevelt's wealthy friends told him not to go into politics because it was "a dirty business." Roosevelt's answer was that it didn't have to be dirty. A man could be a politician and work honestly for the welfare of his country. He joined a Republican club and at twenty-three was elected to the state legislature. Within six weeks he was trying to get a crooked judge thrown out of office. He didn't succeed, but he won a reputation as a fearless and honest legislator.

In 1884 Roosevelt's young wife and his mother both died within a few hours of each other. To forget his grief, Roosevelt moved to the Dakota Territory. He bought a ranch and for two years worked as a cowboy. He spent long days in the saddle. He even became a deputy sheriff and helped hunt down outlaws. Soon he was known for being as fearless on the frontier as in the legislature. Later he said, "There were all kinds of things of which I was afraid at first . . . from grizzly bears to 'mean' horses and gunfighters; but by acting as if I were not afraid, I gradually ceased to be afraid."

After two years Roosevelt went back east. He married again. He served in Washington on the Civil Service Commission and in New York City as commissioner of police. In 1897 President McKinley appointed him assistant secretary of the navy.

At this time Cuba was fighting to become independent of Spain. Roosevelt wanted the United States to join in. He said McKinley was "lily-livered" for not asking Congress to declare war on Spain.

When war was finally declared, Roosevelt quit his government job. He had always been a little ashamed that his own father had not fought in the Civil War. Now he formed a cavalry regiment called the Rough Riders. In it were wealthy polo players from the East and hard-riding cowboys from the West. In Cuba, Roosevelt led them in a charge up San Juan Hill to capture a Spanish fort (see p. 86). Years later he would say, "San Juan was the greatest day of my life."

After the Spanish-American War, Roosevelt was elected governor of New York. He was a strong governor and an honest one. Many professional politicians were afraid of him. It was for this reason that in 1900 they nominated him for Vice President. They thought that as Vice President he would be out of the way with little to do. But on September 6, 1901, President McKinley was shot and killed. Roosevelt was mountain climbing, but he rushed back to take the oath of office as President.

"Now look," one of his enemies moaned, "that damned cowboy is President of the United States."

When McKinley was assassinated, Roosevelt was forty-three—the youngest man ever to become President. And certainly he was one of the most colorful. He was a showman. His favorite word was "Bully!" which meant "wonderful." Whatever Teddy Roosevelt did, he had a bully time doing it.

And being President was bulliest of all.

With all his heart Roosevelt believed in a strong and unified country. But during the presidential election he had seen that the nation was in danger of breaking up. The division then was not between North and South, but between the rich and the poor. At that time, the average working person could earn only between $400 and $500 a year. Part of the reason was that many big businesses were joining to form "trusts." The trusts could kill off any competition. They could force people to work for them at low wages or prevent them from working at all.

Roosevelt was proud of what American big business could produce. But he saw that small businesses and workers needed protection. People called him a "trust buster." Roosevelt said he did not want to "bust the trusts" but only to control them. He wanted everybody to have a "square deal." Because of this his administra-

The original Teddy bear, which was named for Teddy Roosevelt and was presented to him in 1903.

tion became known as the Square Deal. He forced the railroads to give fair rates to small businesses. He forced the owners of coal mines to pay better wages. He forced Congress to pass laws protecting the people from impure food and drugs.

Many professional politicians did not like Roosevelt, but the people did. He was one of the most popular Presidents ever. In 1904 he was reelected by a huge majority.

No President has done more to save the natural resources of the country for the people than Roosevelt. He established national parks and more than 125 million acres of national forests.

Roosevelt believed in a strong navy. He got Congress to build new battleships and cruisers. In international affairs, Roosevelt said, the President should "speak softly and carry a big stick." Roosevelt's own "big stick" was a powerful navy. He sent it on a cruise around the world to show American strength.

Roosevelt also wanted a canal across the Isthmus of Panama. The canal would allow the navy to move rapidly from one ocean to the other. At this time the isthmus belonged to Colombia. Roosevelt tried to buy the land for the canal, but the Colombian government hesitated to sell.

Some of the businessmen in the isthmus who wanted the canal began to plot a revolution. They had the help of U.S. Army officers. Roosevelt also knew about the plan. He sent his warships to the area. When the revolution started, American sailors stopped the Colombian government from sending troops to put down the revolution. Two days later the United States recognized the new Republic of Panama. Then the new country leased part of

its land to the United States for the canal.

Later, enemies of Roosevelt would say he had actually caused the revolution in Panama. The truth is, he did not cause it; but he certainly helped it along to get what he wanted. Roosevelt said he was more proud of the Panama Canal than of anything else done during his administration. He refused to run for a third term. Instead he went big game hunting in Africa. He toured Europe. He wrote books and made speeches. Still, it was not quite enough to keep him busy. He was unhappy with the way the new President, Taft, was running the country, and in 1912 Roosevelt once more ran for President. Since Taft was the Republican candidate, Roosevelt formed a new party, called the Progressive party.

While in Milwaukee to make a campaign speech, Roosevelt was shot by an insane man. He was only wounded and finished his speech before going to the hospital. When a reporter asked how he felt, Roosevelt said, "I feel as strong as a bull moose." From that time on his party was known as the Bull Moose party.

In this election the Republican vote was split between Taft and Roosevelt. And so the Democratic candidate, Woodrow Wilson, was elected.

Roosevelt went back to his home on Long Island. He wrote his autobiography. He wrote magazine articles. He went to South America and spent months exploring an unknown river called the River of Doubt. He got a jungle fever and almost died.

By now he was blind in one eye. He would never be really well again. But when World War I started he wanted to raise a regiment and go to France to fight. President Wilson refused. He wanted the war run by professional military men—and Roosevelt never forgave him.

Less than two years later Roosevelt died quietly in his sleep. It was one of the few things he ever did quietly.

A cartoon of Roosevelt overseeing the digging of the Panama Canal. Note his namesake behind him.

WILLIAM TAFT

27th President of the United States, 1909–1913

Born: September 15, 1857, in Cincinnati, Ohio
Died: March 8, 1930, in Washington, D.C.

Even as a boy William Taft was big. His brothers and sisters called him Big Lub. Other people called him Big Bill. He grew to be about six feet tall and weighed close to three hundred pounds. He was a good tennis player and an excellent dancer. He liked to ride horseback, if he had a horse that could carry him.

Taft's father was a successful lawyer, active in Republican politics. His wife's father had been the law partner of President Rutherford B. Hayes. Their friends urged Big Bill Taft to go into politics, but he was more interested in law. He was a good lawyer. In 1887 the governor of Ohio appointed Taft to the state supreme court. He liked being a judge. The next year he ran for the office of judge and was elected.

In 1901 Taft was appointed civil governor of the Philippines, which then belonged to the United States. He made a good governor. He liked the Filipi-

nos, and they liked him. Then in 1904 President Theodore Roosevelt appointed Taft secretary of war. He did an excellent job. Roosevelt was often away, but everything was all right in Washington, Roosevelt said, because Big Bill Taft was "sitting on the lid."

Roosevelt admired Taft's ability. It was largely because of Roosevelt that the Republican party nominated Taft for President in 1908. Taft, however, was not happy about the idea. He didn't think he would make a good President. His ambition was to be appointed to the Supreme Court. But Mrs. Taft wanted to be First Lady. She talked Taft into running for President. With Roosevelt's backing, he was elected.

Taft planned to carry out Roosevelt's progressive policies. And actually he did a pretty good job of it. He improved the civil service. He was the first President to put aside government-owned lands where oil and coal had been found. He said the profit from these should belong to the people, not to private business.

But Taft simply could not do things with Roosevelt's flair and flash. Roosevelt and many of his followers began to think Taft was not doing enough. Taft himself believed that the powers of the President should be limited. He did not believe that a President, even in a good cause, should take over powers normally given to Congress. He kept framed on his desk a saying by Lincoln: "I do the very best I know how—the very best I can; and I mean to keep on doing so until the end."

Roosevelt and his friends said that Taft had sold out Roosevelt's ideals. When the Republicans nominated Taft to run for a second term in 1912, Roosevelt formed the Bull Moose party to run against him. The Democrats nominated Woodrow Wilson.

Taft was deeply hurt by the things Roosevelt said about him. And he had never liked to campaign. He knew that in a three-way race against Wilson and Roosevelt he had no chance. But he had been nominated, and he did his best.

In the election Roosevelt got more votes than Taft. But Wilson got more than either of them and was elected.

Taft had been one of the most unhappy Presidents. When he left the White House, he said: "I am glad to be going. This is the lonesomest place in the world." He went back to his law practice. He taught law at Yale. Then in 1921 he was appointed Chief Justice of the United States. This was the work he loved. He served until his retirement because of ill health in 1930. "I don't even remember that I ever was President," he said happily.

Taft was the only President to keep cows on the White House lawn.

WOODROW WILSON

28th President of the United States, 1913–1921

Born: December 29, 1856, in Staunton, Virginia
Died: February 3, 1924, in Washington, D.C.

Woodrow Wilson was born in Virginia five years before the start of the Civil War. His father and grandfather were Presbyterian preachers. At one time his father's church was turned into a hospital for wounded Confederate soldiers. All his life Wilson was proud of the gallant fight the South had made. At the same time he was glad the North had won and kept the Union undivided.

With his family and close friends, Wilson was warm, witty, and loving. To many other persons he seemed cold and even bitter. He often told people what he thought was wrong with them and turned friends into enemies.

Wilson had a high forehead, a long, thin nose, and a firm mouth. He looked like a teacher or a preacher. He was not a big man, but he was lean and strong. At Princeton he played football and later he helped coach the team. He received a law degree and for a lit-

tle while practiced law in Atlanta. But he did not like law. He went back to school, received a Ph.D., and began to teach. In 1902 he was made president of Princeton University.

At Princeton, Wilson wanted to do away with the "eating clubs." These were small social groups like fraternities. Wilson did not think they were democratic. He wanted to change Princeton, he said, from "a place where there are youngsters doing tasks to a place where there are men thinking." Not all his reforms were accepted, but Wilson became known as a man who believed in honest, democratic government. In 1910 he was elected governor of New Jersey. Two years later he was elected President.

Like Theodore Roosevelt, Wilson believed the job of the President was to represent all the people. Congressmen, he said, represented special areas and groups. There was no one but the

President "to look out for the general interests of the whole country."

Wilson got Congress to lower the tariff. This angered some big manufacturers, but it brought lower prices to the public. He reformed the national banking system. He got Congress to declare that it was not against federal law for working men to go on strike, as some big businesses had claimed it was.

Wilson had been in office less than two years when World War I began in Europe. It was Wilson's great hope that the United States could stay out. He tried to find ways to help the warring countries make peace.

In 1916 Wilson was nominated for a second term. During the campaign one of the slogans was "He kept us out of war." It helped Wilson win reelection. But soon German submarines began to sink American ships in the Atlantic Ocean without warning. Many lives were lost.

Wilson finally asked Congress to declare war against Germany.

Wilson hoped with all his heart that this would be a "war to end all wars." Even while the fighting was going on he drew up his famous Fourteen Points peace plan. The most important point called for a League of Nations. This would be an impartial organization that would represent every country. Wilson hoped that such a league could settle all future arguments between nations.

In November 1918 Germany surrendered and the fighting in Europe stopped. The League of Nations was soon formed. But the United States could not join unless the U.S. Senate approved.

Wilson for President buttons

The four leaders who negotiated the Treaty of Versailles (signed in June 1919), which ended World War I. From left to right: Prime Minister Lloyd George of England, Premier Clemenceau of France, Premier Orlando of Italy, and Wilson.

Some senators did not want the United States to join at all. Many others wanted to join, but only if certain changes were made in the league plan. If Wilson had agreed to the changes, the Senate would have passed the bill. But Wilson refused to make any compromise. Instead, he started on a trip around the country making speeches in favor of the league.

For many months he had been working long hours, day and night, under great strain. Now, suddenly, he became too sick to go on. He had a stroke that paralyzed his left side. For two months he was hardly conscious. No one except his doctor, his secretary, and his family could see him. His wife, Edith, was his link to the outside world. She read government reports for Wilson, screened his visitors, and relayed his decisions. Probably no other First Lady had more influence on the presidency than she did. This angered some members of Congress. One senator said, "We have a petticoat government! Mrs. Wilson is President!"

Without Wilson's leadership the U.S. Senate voted against joining the League of Nations. And without the United States the league was of little value.

Gradually Wilson recovered some of

his strength. But he was never really well again. After his second term in office was over, he took no more part in politics. But others would continue to fight for his ideals and the hope of a world without war.

Edith Bolling Galt Wilson

WARREN HARDING

29th President of the United States, 1921–1923

Born: November 2, 1865, in Corsica, Ohio
Died: August 2, 1923, in San Francisco, California

Warren Harding was raised in small Ohio towns. He was a tall, handsome, bright boy. Everybody liked him. He quit school at seventeen, taught briefly in a country school, and got a job on a weekly newspaper in Marion, Ohio, called the *Democratic Mirror*. A year or so later he and two friends bought a bankrupt weekly paper called the *Star*.

The town of Marion was growing, and the paper grew with it. Harding married the daughter of the local banker. He made money.

A few years later he ran for governor and was defeated. But in 1914 he was elected to the United States Senate.

Harding liked being a senator. He didn't worry too much about the big national problems. He was a loyal Republican and usually voted the way he was told. He was also loyal to his friends back home. He spent most of his time trying to find jobs for them. He was so busy at it that he missed half the roll calls in the Senate.

One of Harding's friends was a politician named Harry Daugherty. Daugherty set out to see if he could get Harding elected President.

At the Republican convention in 1920 the votes were split among three important candidates. Nobody could get enough votes to be nominated. So a number of powerful politicians met Daugherty in "a smoke-filled room" in a local hotel. They all knew Harding. They liked him; everybody liked him.

At two o'clock in the morning they agreed to support Harding. So he got the nomination.

World War I had been over for only two years. The American people were weary of wartime problems and shortages. They blamed Europe for the war, and they wanted no more to do with it.

Harding promised a "return to normalcy." He won the election in a land-slide.

As President, Harding wanted to do something for world peace. He called a disarmament conference in Washington. There Charles Hughes, the secretary of state, worked out a plan for limiting the world's navies. This was probably the most important action of Harding's administration.

Unfortunately, not all the men Harding appointed were either honest or capable. He made Daugherty attorney general. And he brought in so many of his old Ohio pals that in Washington they became known as the Ohio Gang. Some of these men had little ability. Others were outright crooks. They set out to get rich off the government.

No one can be sure just how much Harding knew about what his friends were doing. He must have had some idea. But he did nothing about it.

Then, in August 1923, he suddenly became ill. A few days later he died.

Then the stories began to come out. The most famous of these became known as the Teapot Dome scandal. The secretary of the interior had rented publicly owned oil fields to private companies in exchange for over three million dollars in bribes. For this he was sent to prison.

A campaign ribbon for Harding

Some other members of the Ohio Gang went to jail and some committed suicide rather than face trial. And as the people learned about how crooked Harding's administration had been, they began to wonder about the President's sudden illness and death. Soon rumors said he had killed himself. Other rumors said his wife had poisoned him. The exact truth was never known. But now it seems probable that he died of a heart attack.

CALVIN COOLIDGE

30th President of the United States, 1923–1929

Born: July 4, 1872, in Plymouth Notch, Vermont
Died: January 5, 1933, in Northampton, Massachusetts

Calvin Coolidge was raised in Vermont where his father had a country store and small farm. He graduated from Amherst College and practiced law in Northampton, Massachusetts. When he went into politics he was elected to the state legislature. He came back to Northampton to be mayor and then was elected lieutenant governor in 1916, governor in 1918.

Calvin Coolidge was not a typical, back-slapping politician. He had a lean, sour look. His mouth turned down at the corners. It shut as tight as a clamshell, and he didn't open it any more than he needed to. When he made speeches they were short and to the point. He became known as Silent Cal.

Coolidge worked hard. He gave people the impression of being safe, conservative, and totally honest. Each time he ran for office he got more votes than the time before.

Coolidge first drew national atten-

tion while he was governor of Massachusetts. In 1919 the police in Boston went on strike. Coolidge promptly called out the entire National Guard and broke the strike. "There is no right to strike against the public safety by anybody, anywhere, at any time," he said. Largely because of this action, he was nominated by the Republicans for Vice President in 1920. He was elected with President Harding.

When Harding died suddenly in 1923, Coolidge was visiting his father. He was awakened by a messenger in the middle of the night and told that he was now President. By the light of a kerosene lamp, his hand on the old family Bible, Coolidge took the oath of office from his father, who was a justice of the peace.

The scandals of the Harding administration were not yet public. When they did become known, they did not bother Coolidge. Even the Democrats never suspected Coolidge of being dishonest.

Coolidge said that "the business of America is business." And the business of government was to keep out of business. "When things are going all right," he said, "it is a good plan to let them alone."

Things seemed to be going very well indeed. Business was booming.

People were gambling on the stock market, and stocks were going up. Prices were going up. Wages were going up. And Coolidge was tremendously popular. He made people feel safe. He never gambled a nickel and never spent a nickel that he didn't have to. He is probably the only President who ever saved money from his salary.

He was no more talkative as President than he had been before. Once a young lady sitting next to him at a White House dinner said, "Mr. President, I have made a bet I can get more than three words out of you during the meal."

Without even looking at her he said, "You lose."

Sitting on top of flagpoles for long periods of time was a craze while Coolidge was President. This 1927 flagpole sitter is Alvin "Shipwreck" Kelly.

In 1924 Coolidge was elected President in his own right. Probably he could have been elected again in 1928. But he said, "I do not choose to run." Some historians believe he did not really mean it, but the voters believed it. At the end of his term he retired.

This was lucky for Coolidge. Around the country a few people had been saying that unless something was done to slow down the economic boom, it was sure to break and bring on a depression. Coolidge did not believe them. He took no action.

A few months later the boom did break. The country was plunged into the most terrible depression of its history. Millions of people lost their jobs, their homes, and their life savings. Many committed suicide because they were ruined financially. Coolidge did not understand. He kept thinking times ought to get better. And instead they got worse. Shortly before his death in 1933 he said, "I no longer fit in with these times."

During Coolidge's presidency Charles Lindbergh became the first person to fly alone nonstop across the Atlantic Ocean. In May 1927, Lindbergh flew his single-engine plane, *The Spirit of St. Louis* (shown here), from New York City to Paris. The trip took 33 hours, 29 minutes, and 30 seconds.

HERBERT HOOVER

31st President of the United States, 1929–1933

Born: August 10, 1874, in West Branch, Iowa
Died: October 20, 1964, in New York City

Herbert Hoover was the first President born west of the Mississippi River. His father, a blacksmith in a small Iowa town, died when Herbert was six. His mother, a deeply religious Quaker, supported her three children by preaching and taking in sewing. She died when Herbert was nine. After that he lived with an uncle in Oregon.

The uncle had a real estate office where Herbert worked after school. One day a man who was a mining engineer came in. Herbert heard him talking about his work and how he traveled from one job to another around the world. The boy was deeply impressed. When he was seventeen he went to Stanford University to study engineering.

After graduation Hoover worked in San Francisco. When he was twenty-three he went to Australia. He helped develop one of the richest gold mines in the world. Two years later he came back to California and married his college sweetheart, Lou Henry. By the time Hoover was in his thirties, he was rich.

Hoover was in London when World War I began. Suddenly many Americans who had been traveling abroad could not get money to go home. Hoover formed an organization that helped more than a hundred thousand Americans return from Europe. Much of the money he paid out of his own pocket.

When the German army captured Belgium, many of the Belgian people were without food. Hoover helped bring food from the United States and get it through the German lines. His work saved millions of people from starving.

When America entered the war, President Wilson appointed Hoover the food administrator. His job was to get the American people to save food so it could be sent to the Allies and soldiers in Europe. Hoover had no real power to enforce his rules, but he got people to save food anyway.

Because of this work President Harding appointed Hoover secretary of commerce. He worked as hard at this job as at all his other jobs. One newspaper wrote that Hoover was "the Secretary of Commerce and the Under Secretary of Everything Else."

In 1928 the Republicans nominated Hoover for President. He had never run for any political office. But most Americans knew and honored the work he had done. He was elected by a huge majority.

Then, almost suddenly, the good times ended. In 1929 the stock market crashed and the Great Depression began. Businesses that had borrowed too much money failed. People were out of work. Without jobs they could not buy things. So more businesses failed and put more people out of work. Banks failed and many people lost all they had saved. Hoover was slow to act. A truly kind man, it hurt him to see people hungry. But he felt the government should not interfere with business.

Nobody truly understood what caused the Depression. But because people wanted to blame someone, they blamed Hoover. When people lost their jobs, they said it was Hoover's fault the government did not do enough to help. People who had lost their homes had to live in villages of makeshift shacks that became known as Hoovervilles.

A poor family who set up home in a makeshift tin shack during the Great Depression of 1929

Long "bread lines" of people waiting for jobs and food became common during the Depression.

Finally Hoover established an organization to lend government money to businesses in need. Hoover also started some programs to give people jobs. These helped, but they did not end the Depression. And in the election of 1932 Hoover was overwhelmingly defeated.

Hoover went back to private life. At this time he was hated by many people who thought he was to blame for the Depression. But gradually people understood that no one person was to blame. Then in 1940 the Soviet Union and Finland went to war. Hoover raised great stocks of food to help feed the Finns. After World War II he was named by President Truman to head the Famine Emergency Commission. This commission sent food to people in countries destroyed by war. Once more Hoover's work helped save millions of lives.

FRANKLIN D. ROOSEVELT

32nd President of the United States, 1933–1945

Born: January 30, 1882, in Hyde Park, New York
Died: April 12, 1945, in Warm Springs, Georgia

Franklin Roosevelt was born into a wealthy and well-known family. President Theodore Roosevelt was his fifth cousin. Franklin was also distantly related to ten other Presidents: Washington, both Adamses, Madison, Van Buren, both Harrisons, Taylor, Grant, and Taft.

As a boy, Roosevelt never went to public schools. An only child, he often traveled with his parents in Europe. He learned foreign languages. He had private tutors. When he was fourteen he was sent to Groton, a private school. Later Roosevelt went to Harvard University. He was a tall, lean, good-looking boy. He went out for the football team and the crew. He never made the varsity, though he tried. But all his life he was proud of having been editor of the school paper his senior year.

After Harvard, Roosevelt studied law. He married a distant cousin, named Eleanor Roosevelt. Eleanor's father was

dead, so at the wedding, Franklin's cousin, President Teddy Roosevelt, gave the bride away.

Franklin Roosevelt greatly admired his cousin Teddy. Like Teddy, Franklin believed that politics offered a wealthy man a chance to serve his country. But Teddy was a Republican. Franklin's father was a Democrat. So Franklin joined the Democratic party.

Franklin began his career by running for the New York State Legislature. No one thought he had a chance, because most people in his county were Republicans. Franklin hired a bright red automobile so he could travel and meet the people. To almost everybody's surprise he was elected.

Franklin was delighted when President Wilson appointed him assistant secretary of the navy, a post Teddy Roosevelt had once held. In his new job he worked hard to build a good navy. When World War I began, Roosevelt wanted to quit his job and join the navy as a fighting man. But President Wilson would not let him go. His work as assistant secretary was too important.

After the war Roosevelt was nominated by the Democrats to run for Vice President. Campaigning gave him a chance to meet people all around the country, but he and the presidential candidate, Governor James Cox of Ohio, were defeated.

Then in 1921, something happened to change the whole course of Roosevelt's life. Quite suddenly he became ill with polio. For a while he couldn't move his arms or legs. Slowly, almost by sheer willpower, he fought his way back. He regained the use of his hands and arms. He spent long hours swimming and exercising. He was never again able to walk without braces on his legs and crutches, but he developed very powerful arms and shoulders.

Even while he was sick, Roosevelt kept up his interest in politics. In 1924, walking on crutches, he appeared at the Democratic National Convention to nominate Al Smith for President. Smith was defeated, but he persuaded Roosevelt to run for governor of New York in 1928.

Roosevelt was elected. He was in office when the Great Depression of the 1930s began. All over the country businesses began to fail. Millions of people were out of work. With no jobs they could not buy new houses or automobiles. So more businesses failed, and more people were put out of work. Banks failed and families lost their savings.

As governor of New York, Roosevelt used the power of the state to help businesses and people who were out of work. He talked to the people over

Putting people back to work was one of the major goals of Roosevelt's New Deal legislation.

the radio. He called these talks fireside chats, and in them he told the people what he was trying to do.

Partly because of these talks, the Democrats nominated Roosevelt for President in 1932. Herbert Hoover, the Republican President, was running for a second term. Many people blamed Hoover for the Depression. This was not fair, but it helped Roosevelt to win.

By the time Roosevelt took office, the Depression had grown still worse. More than five thousand banks had failed. Not only were people out of work, but many were hungry and waited in long lines, called bread lines, for food. Many had lost their homes.

Roosevelt took action. First he declared a bank holiday. This closed all the banks so no more could fail. Then the banks were reopened a few at a time with government help. Roosevelt asked for new laws to help the farmers and small businessmen. He asked for laws to help people about to lose their homes.

Quickly Congress passed the laws Roosevelt asked for. As one congressman said, "The house is burning down and the President of the United States says this is the way to put out the fire."

Roosevelt said, "The only thing we have to fear is fear itself." And the President's own confidence made the people more confident. He had a big grin and a booming laugh. He smoked cigarettes in a long holder and held it cocked at an angle in the corner of his mouth.

Roosevelt found it difficult to travel, so often Mrs. Roosevelt traveled for him. She went everywhere. She talked to people all over the country, then went home to tell the President what was needed. Eleanor Roosevelt became the best known and most widely loved of all the First Ladies.

Franklin and Eleanor Roosevelt returning from his inauguration in January 1941

In the election of 1936 Franklin Roosevelt carried every state in the Union except two. He kept on with his social reforms. Gradually times got better.

Teddy Roosevelt had called his administration the Square Deal. His cousin Franklin Roosevelt called his administration the New Deal. He believed in using the full power of the government to help what he called the forgotten man. By this he meant the small businessman, the worker, the wage earner. And it was these people who came to love him most deeply. They felt that they knew him personally.

On the other hand there were many who honestly believed that Roosevelt's methods were destroying the American system of government. They hated him in the same intense way that other people loved him. Many people would not even say his name. They called Roosevelt "that madman in the White House."

By 1939 Roosevelt and the nation had a new problem to face. World War II began in Europe. Roosevelt, like most Americans, wanted the Allies to win. At the same time he hoped America could stay out of the war. As one country after another was defeated by the Germans, Roosevelt sent more and more supplies to the British.

In 1940 the Democrats nominated Roosevelt for a third term. No President had ever served three terms, not even Washington. Many people believed no President should serve more than twice, although there was no law against it at that time. But Roosevelt did not want to quit while the nation was in danger. He loved power and he enjoyed being President. He accepted the nomination and won an easy victory.

On December 7, 1941, the Japanese bombed Pearl Harbor in Hawaii and America was plunged into the war.

The United States Pacific fleet in flames at Pearl Harbor, December 7, 1941

Roosevelt holds the declaration of war against Japan that he has just signed. He wears a black armband in mourning for the Americans killed at Pearl Harbor.

Now there were tremendous decisions to be made. Roosevelt met often with Winston Churchill, the British prime minister, and with other Allied leaders. They made the plans for war around the world.

In 1944 the war was still going on. Roosevelt was elected for the fourth time. But now the terrible strain and the long hours of work were destroying his health. His face had a gray look. Then his famous smile would flash and he would look strong again.

But President Roosevelt had enough energy to start another major project. He played an important part in setting up another world organization. In the summer and fall of 1944 representatives of the United States, Great Britain, the Soviet Union, and Nationalist China met at Dumbarton Oaks, in Washington, D.C. They drafted plans for what became known as the United Nations. Its charter was drawn up the next year (when Truman was President) in San Francisco.

On April 12, 1945, Roosevelt was resting at his cottage in Warm Springs, Georgia. An artist was painting his picture. Suddenly he put a hand to his head and fell backward in his chair. A few hours later he was dead.

All over the world people from every walk of life mourned the President. In Europe, on ships at sea, in the jungles of the South Pacific, soldiers and sailors wept openly. As one sailor said, "It's tough when one of your buddies has to go, and President Roosevelt was our buddy." Many millions of people felt the same way.

U.S. Marines raising the American flag on the Pacific island of Iwo Jima, after one of the bloodiest battles of World War II

HARRY S TRUMAN

33rd President of the United States, 1945–1953

Born: May 8, 1884, in Lamar, Missouri
Died: December 26, 1972, in Kansas City, Missouri

As a child, Harry Truman was often sick. By the time he was eight years old he had to wear glasses. He was so afraid he might break them that he rarely took part in the rough games of other boys. Instead he spent much of his time reading. Before he was fourteen, he said later, he had read every book in the library in Independence, Missouri, where the family then lived.

Truman did not go to college. He worked for a railroad, at a bank, and on the family farm. He was thirty-three when World War I began. He promptly volunteered and went to France as a captain of artillery.

When the war was over he came home and married his childhood sweetheart. Then he and a friend started a men's clothing store in Kansas City. It failed. Truman could have declared bankruptcy and paid only part of what he owed. Instead, he paid off all his debts.

Because he was out of a job, Truman decided to go into politics. At this time the most powerful politician in Missouri was a man named Tom Pendergast. Much later Pendergast would be sent to prison for cheating on his income tax as well as fixing elections. But at this time it was almost impossible to be elected in Truman's home county without Pendergast's help. Truman asked for Pendergast's help and got it. He was elected county judge—a job that in most states would be called county commissioner. He attracted statewide attention by making sure —to most people's surprise—that the roads in his county were built honestly.

In 1934 Truman was elected to the U.S. Senate, again with Pendergast's help. When World War II began, he became chairman of a committee. The committee was to oversee how government funds were spent on supplies. Truman did an excellent job that saved the country more than a billion dollars.

When Roosevelt ran for his fourth term in 1944, there were several important men who wanted to be Vice President. Roosevelt did not want to choose between them so he asked that Truman be nominated instead. But after the election Roosevelt gave Truman very little to do. Roosevelt didn't even bother to tell him much about what was going on.

Then, suddenly, Roosevelt died and Truman was President.

All over the country people wondered how Truman would do as President. Back in Missouri he had been elected with the help of one of the nation's most crooked political groups. Now would he be loyal to the group or to his country?

For Truman himself there was never any doubt. He loved his country. He was fiercely proud of it. He was stunned by the size of the job facing him, but he was determined to do his best.

The war in Europe ended less than a month after Truman took office. He went to Europe to help draw up the peace. He had help with this job, but on the way home he was faced with one of the most terrible decisions anyone has ever had to make. The United States had developed the atom bomb. Should it be used on Japan or not? The President had to decide. The war with Japan was still going on in the Pacific. Japan still controlled China and a number of islands. It is almost certain that if the bomb had not been used, the United States would have had to invade Japan. Many more people, Americans as well as Japanese, would have been killed in the fighting.

Truman gave orders to drop the bomb. Two Japanese cities, Hiroshima and Nagasaki, were destroyed before Japan surrendered.

After the war Truman asked Congress to pass civil rights laws and to increase Social Security. That is a system of monthly payments to retired and disabled people. It had been started as part of Franklin Roosevelt's New Deal. But Congress rarely passed the laws Truman asked for.

In 1948 Truman ran for President against Thomas E. Dewey, the governor of New York. The newspapers and the polls predicted Truman would be badly defeated. But Truman traveled back and forth across the country. He made more than 350 speeches. And to almost everyone's surprise, he won.

World War II was over, but the Cold War with the Soviet Union had begun. Once more Truman was faced with tremendous decisions. The Russians tried to force the other Allies out of Berlin by blocking the roads and railroads across Russian-held territory. Truman ordered supplies flown in. For months the Berlin airlift, as it was called, brought in everything from food to coal. Finally the Russians gave in and opened the roads.

Communists tried to overthrow the government of Greece. Truman declared that the United States would help countries fighting to stay free of Communism. This was called the Truman Doctrine. It helped Greece and other countries. Under Truman's leadership the United States helped free European countries rebuild houses and factories that had been destroyed in the war.

After the war Korea had been divided into two parts. The northern half was under Communist control; the southern half was supposed to be

Truman triumphantly holds a newspaper that was printed before his upset victory in the presidential campaign of 1948.

democratic. In June 1950, Communists from northern Korea invaded the south. Truman immediately ordered American troops to go to Korea. Then he asked for and got the help of the newly formed United Nations to save South Korea.

People who did not like Truman said he was not dignified enough to be President. He did swear a lot. He liked to play poker and he lost his temper too easily. But history has shown that on the big decisions Harry Truman was nearly always right. And he faced some of the most awesome decisions of any American President.

DWIGHT D. EISENHOWER

34th President of the United States, 1953–1961

Born: October 14, 1890, in Denison, Texas
Died: March 28, 1969, in Washington, D.C.

Young Dwight Eisenhower had his heart set on going to the Naval Academy at Annapolis. He wanted to be a sailor. But the examination he took to enter Annapolis was the same required for the army school at West Point. So on his paper he had to mark one of three choices: army, navy, or either.

Eisenhower marked the word *either*. When his appointment came through, it was to West Point.

At West Point, Eisenhower played football until he hurt his knee. He was not big, but he was fast, lean, and hard. He had a big grin and great personal charm. His teammates called him by his nickname, Ike. His class grades were average.

During World War I, Eisenhower was a training officer in the United States. Later he served on the staffs of General John Pershing and General Douglas MacArthur. When World War II be-

gan he was asked to draw up plans for war in the Pacific. These were so good that President Roosevelt promoted him over 366 other officers to head the U.S. armies in Europe. Soon he was made commander of all the Allied Forces in Europe.

This was a job that called for much more than just military skill. Eisenhower had to get along with generals from half a dozen countries. Also, he had to get along with the politicians who headed these countries. It was his skill, tact, and great personal charm that made him so successful in this job.

After the war Eisenhower retired from the army and was appointed president of Columbia University. In 1948 both political parties wanted him to run for President. He refused. He said he did not believe a professional military man should be President.

The politicians kept after him. And

General Eisenhower talking to American paratroopers before the Allied invasion of Normandy, France, during World War II

in 1952 he agreed to run on the Republican ticket.

Eisenhower was not a good public speaker. He sometimes stumbled over his words. His sentences got tangled up. But it was obvious that he was to-tally honest. He had a big grin that made people feel they knew him personally. And everybody liked him. Even people who usually voted Democratic wore buttons that said I LIKE IKE. He won an easy victory to become the first

Republican President in twenty years.

Eisenhower's great hope was that as President he could work for peace. He had seen enough war, he said. Now he would fight for peace.

At this time the war in Korea was still going on. American and United Nations forces were still fighting the Communists. Right after his election Eisenhower flew to Korea. It was largely through his efforts that peace was achieved a few months later.

Eisenhower tried hard to find some way to get along better with the Russians. He wanted to end the danger of war. He said America would stop testing atomic weapons if the Russians would too. He set up a plan called Atoms for Peace to help smaller nations. Few of these ideas worked, because the Russians would not agree.

At home Eisenhower did not make many changes in the policies begun by Presidents Roosevelt and Truman. He broadened the Social Security system and the minimum wage law. He started a new system of national highways.

In 1955 Eisenhower had a heart attack. But he recovered quickly and the following year was elected to a second term by a huge majority.

Eisenhower believed wholeheartedly in equal rights for all citizens. He completed the integration of the armed forces started by Roosevelt and Truman. He asked Congress for new civil rights laws. He did not, however, work as hard for these and other laws as Roosevelt and Truman had. Because of this he was not regarded as a "strong" President. But when the opportunity came, he made his position clear. When the governor of Arkansas refused to obey the law to integrate the high school in Little Rock, Eisenhower called out the army and forced the governor to obey.

It was during Eisenhower's administration that an important new program got under way. On October 4, 1957, the Soviet Union shocked the world by launching the first artificial

Eisenhower campaign buttons

118

Eisenhower was an avid golfer. It was largely because of him that the sport became nationally popular. Here he and Vice President Nixon walk between holes at a golf course in Denver, Colorado.

satellite into space. It was called *Sputnik*. Many Americans had believed the United States was superior to the Soviet Union in technology. *Sputnik* seemed to shatter that belief. On January 31, 1958, *Explorer I*, the first American satellite, was launched. And so a "space race" between the two nations began.

At the end of his second term Eisenhower was seventy years old, the oldest man till that time ever to be President. He was happy to retire to a farm he had bought near Gettysburg, Pennsylvania. Because so much of his life had been spent in the army, it was the first home he and Mrs. Eisenhower had ever owned. He lived there until his death in 1969.

JOHN F. KENNEDY

35th President of the United States, 1961–1963

Born: May 29, 1917, in Brookline, Massachusetts
Died: November 22, 1963, in Dallas, Texas

John Kennedy's father, Joseph Kennedy, was a businessman who made a huge fortune. Joseph Kennedy had nine children (John was the second oldest) and he gave each of them a million dollars when they became twenty-one. He also planned what his sons should do. Joseph Kennedy, Jr., the oldest boy, was to be the family politician. John—his family called him Jack—was to be a writer and teacher. He went to Harvard.

When World War II began, John Kennedy joined the navy. He was the skipper of a PT boat in the South Pacific. During a night battle a Japanese destroyer rammed into his small boat, cutting it in half. Two men were killed and Kennedy's back was badly hurt. Despite his own injury, Kennedy swam for hours, towing another man even more badly hurt to a nearby island.

Joseph Kennedy, Jr., the brother who had planned to go into politics, was

killed during the war. So the family decided that John would take his place. He ran for Congress from Massachusetts—and the whole family pitched in to help. His brothers and sisters made speeches. They gave teas and invited thousands of people. They made thousands of telephone calls.

Kennedy was elected easily. He served three terms in the House of Representatives. Then he was elected to the Senate.

The wartime injury to Kennedy's back was still bothering him and he had to have an operation. While he was getting well he wrote a book called *Profiles in Courage* about United States senators who had risked their careers to fight for things they believed in. It won a prize for the best American history book of that year.

From the first, Kennedy had planned to run for President. In 1956 he tried for the Democratic vice presidential

Left: Nine-year-old John Kennedy as a football player on the Dexter School team. "I wasn't a terribly good athlete but I participated," he said.

Below: Kennedy as a naval lieutenant in World War II. When his PT boat was sunk by Japanese fire, he rescued his crew despite agonizing pain from his bad back. Kennedy saved one man by swimming for five hours with the strap of the crewman's life jacket between his teeth.

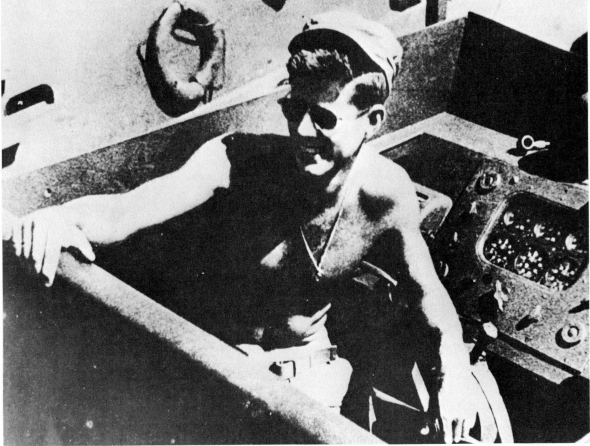

The Kennedy family enjoyed great national popularity. Here, from left to right, is the President with his son, John, Jr.; wife, Jacqueline; and daughter, Caroline.

nomination but lost. Right away he started working toward the next election. As usual, his whole family helped. Since they were all wealthy, money was no problem. They traveled back and forth across the country. They made speeches and talked with politicians. John Kennedy himself worked hardest of all. And when the Democratic Convention met, he was nominated for President on the first ballot.

Kennedy was forty-three years old. Many people thought Kennedy was too young. They thought he did not have enough experience. If elected, he would also be the first Catholic President. Some people did not like that. But for the first time during a presidential campaign the candidates, Kennedy and Richard Nixon, debated with each other on television. This was a big help to Kennedy. He not only was handsome but had great personal charm. He was also smart. He studied hard and had his facts ready. He spoke well and did not get flustered.

The election was one of the closest in history, but Kennedy won.

As President, Kennedy brought many teachers, writers, and scientists into the government. Many of them worked for less money than they had made before. But they were willing to do this because they admired Kennedy. They believed in the things he wanted to do.

President Kennedy established the Peace Corps to help underdeveloped countries. He worked hard for new civil rights laws. He wanted to improve United States relations with Latin America. Congress, however, did not approve of most of Kennedy's plans.

Kennedy hoped the United States could have more friendly relations with the Soviet Union. At first, however, things got worse instead of better. Cuba, under Fidel Castro, had already turned Communist. Kennedy supported an unsuccessful invasion of Cuba by anti-Castro Cubans and Americans on April 17, 1961. This was called the Bay of Pigs Invasion. It hurt American prestige in Latin America and threatened American-Soviet relations as well.

In October 1962, Kennedy learned that the Russians were sending nuclear missiles to Cuba. This became known as the Cuban Missile Crisis. Americans became especially alarmed because Cuba was so close—only ninety miles from Florida. With atomic warheads in Cuba, the Soviet Union could destroy cities all across the United States.

Kennedy acted promptly. He ordered the navy to blockade Cuba so no more Russian ships could enter. He sent planes and soldiers to Florida to be ready to invade Cuba if necessary. On television he told the American people what had happened. He explained the grave danger of war. He asked the Russian leader, Nikita Khrushchev, "to halt and eliminate this . . . threat to world peace."

For one week the United States and Russia seemed on the edge of war. Then the Russians backed down. They took their missiles out of Cuba. After that, relations with the Soviet Union did become a little better.

On November 22, 1963, Kennedy was to make a speech in Dallas, Texas. As he rode through the street, sitting beside his wife, Jacqueline, he was shot and killed by an assassin's bullets.

The entire nation was stunned at the President's death. Because he was so young and vital, the people mourned him as they had mourned no President since Lincoln.

The riderless horse in Kennedy's funeral procession symbolized the loss of the country's leader.

LYNDON B. JOHNSON

36th President of the United States, 1963–1969

Born: August 27, 1908, near Stonewall, Texas
Died: January 22, 1973, in San Antonio, Texas

It was natural enough for Lyndon Johnson to become a politician. Both his father and grandfather had been members of the Texas Legislature. The day Lyndon was born his grandfather mounted his horse and went galloping around the country. "A United States senator has just been born!" he shouted to his friends.

Lyndon's father and mother were both schoolteachers. They taught Lyndon to read by the time he was four. In school he got good grades. But when he finished high school he felt he had had enough school. He was six feet three inches tall, skinny, and restless. He was always moving, trying to do two or three things at one time. But he did not yet know just what he really wanted to do. So he traveled around the country, working at odd jobs.

Finally he went back home. "I'm sick of working with my hands," he told his parents. "I don't know if I can work with my brain, but I'm ready to try."

He went to college. He got good grades. And he became interested in campus politics. He organized a political party that won all the campus elections.

After college Johnson taught school. But he could not leave politics. He worked for a man named Robert Kleberg who was running for Congress. Kleberg was elected and took Johnson to Washington as his secretary.

Working for Kleberg, Johnson had to travel back and forth to Texas. On one of these trips he met Claudia Taylor. Everybody called her Lady Bird, a nickname given to her when she was two years old. Within a few months Lyndon and Lady Bird were married.

When Johnson was twenty-nine years old he ran for Congress on his own and was elected. A few years later when the Japanese bombed Pearl Harbor, Johnson quickly asked for active duty in the navy. He was the first member of Congress to go into uniform.

After World War II, Johnson was elected to the U.S. Senate. He proved to be one of the best senators in history. He had a great gift for getting people with different ideas to work together.

In 1960 Johnson was elected Vice President along with President Kennedy. When Kennedy was killed on November 22, 1963, Johnson became President. He promised the American people to carry on with Kennedy's plans. He said, "I will do my best. That is all I can do. I ask for your help—and God's."

During his first year as President, Johnson pushed many important bills through Congress. Then in 1964 he was elected President by a huge majority.

Under Johnson's leadership Congress passed new civil rights laws. One of these guaranteed blacks the right to vote. This had been denied them in some southern states. "To deny a man his hopes because of color or race, his religion or place of birth," President Johnson said, "is not only to do injustice, it is to deny America and dishonor the dead who gave their lives for freedom."

Johnson began what he called a War on Poverty to improve city slums and other poor sections of the country. He got Congress to pass a Medicare law. This helped old people pay their medical bills. He saw that laws were passed to slow down the pollution of American rivers and air and to make high-

Right after Kennedy died, Johnson was sworn in as President aboard the presidential plane in Dallas, Texas. From left to right: Judge Sarah Hughes of Dallas, new First Lady Lady Bird Johnson, the new President, and Jacqueline Kennedy.

Johnson shakes hands with Martin Luther King, Jr., after signing the Civil Rights Act of 1964, which prohibited racial discrimination in voting, education, and other areas.

ways more beautiful. These laws were supposed to help build the "Great Society"—what Johnson wanted for all Americans.

Not everyone approved of the laws Johnson passed. Many conservatives said that the civil rights laws gave blacks too many rights. Many liberals and blacks themselves believed that the laws did not go far enough. Race riots broke out in a number of cities be-

cause of these conflicts.

In foreign affairs the big problem that faced Johnson was in Southeast Asia. Since the end of World War II, Communist revolutionaries supported by the North Vietnamese government had tried to overthrow the government of South Vietnam, an American ally. President Eisenhower had sent American soldiers to advise the South Vietnamese soldiers. President

Kennedy had sent more advisers and military supplies, too. But South Vietnam continued to lose the war. So President Johnson sent even more soldiers and supplies. These soldiers fought alongside the South Vietnamese troops against the North Vietnamese. Many American soldiers were killed or wounded in the fighting. At home Johnson's Great Society programs began to suffer because so much money and attention were going to the war in Vietnam.

Many Americans thought the United States had no business in Vietnam. They wanted Johnson to bring the soldiers home. Other Americans said the fight in Vietnam was part of our worldwide fight against Communism. They wanted Johnson to send a huge army to South Vietnam. They wanted North Vietnam bombed off the map so that the war would end.

Johnson's stand was in the middle. He did not want to destroy North Vietnam. He did not want to start a nuclear war with the Soviet Union, North Vietnam's ally. Time and again he tried to make peace, but only if the North Vietnamese would retreat from the south. And the Communists would not agree.

Because of the racial problems at home and the war in Vietnam—especially because of the war—the people of the United States grew more and more divided. They grew angry at one another and at the President. At first Johnson had been a popular President, but now he became one of the most disliked. He was especially criticized by young people. They staged huge demonstrations across the country to protest the war. They burned American flags and army draft cards. Johnson was trying to do what he thought best for the whole country and was terribly hurt by the violent criticism.

On March 31, 1968, Johnson made a television speech that surprised the country. He said he had always hoped to lead a united nation, because a country divided against itself could not survive. But now the country was badly divided. In such times, Johnson said, he did not believe a President should devote his time to a political campaign. Therefore, he said, "I shall not seek, and I will not accept, the nomination of my party for another term as your President."

Johnson retired to his Texas ranch when his term was over in 1969. Four years later he died of a heart attack.

RICHARD M. NIXON

37th President of the United States, 1969–1974

Born: January 9, 1913, in Yorba Linda, California
Died: April 22, 1994, in New York City

Richard Nixon was still a small boy when his parents moved from Yorba Linda to Whittier, California. There his father ran a grocery store and a small filling station. Richard worked in both. Often he got up at four in the morning to go into the nearby city of Los Angeles to buy fresh vegetables for the grocery. Then he was back home and ready for school by eight o'clock.

Nixon was a good student and got good grades. He graduated from Whittier College, a small college near his home, and then won a scholarship to Duke University, in North Carolina, where he studied law. He went back to California to practice, but when World War II started he joined the navy.

After the war Nixon was asked to run for Congress on the Republican ticket in California. His district usually elected a Democrat, and few people thought Nixon could win. But he worked hard and he did win. He served two terms in the House of Representatives and then was elected to the Senate. In 1952, presidential candidate Dwight Eisenhower selected Richard Nixon as his running mate. Eisenhower and Nixon were elected.

Nixon spent most of his time as Vice President traveling to fifty-six different countries representing the United States government. When Eisenhower got sick, Nixon served as acting President.

In 1960 Nixon ran for President against John Kennedy. He was defeated in one of the closest elections in history. He went back to California and ran for governor. Again he was defeated. Nixon blamed the press for his loss. He told reporters, "You won't have Nixon to kick around anymore, because, gentlemen, this is my last press conference." Nixon said he would never run for office again. Instead he moved to New York and joined a law firm.

Yet Nixon went right on working with professional Republican politicians. He helped many who were running for office. They in turn helped him get nominated for President in 1968. And this time he won.

His biggest problem was how to end the war in Vietnam. He slowly began to withdraw U.S. ground troops while steadily increasing American bombing of North Vietnam. He established a training program in Vietnam to help the South Vietnamese army defend itself.

At the same time Nixon worked to improve relations with the Communist world. In February 1972 he became the first American President to visit Communist China. This opened new channels for trade and communications. In May he visited Moscow and made plans to reduce the production

History was made in July 1969 when American astronauts Edwin Aldrin (shown here) and Neil Armstrong became the first human beings to walk on the moon. Armstrong and the lunar landing module are reflected in Aldrin's helmet.

At the Great Wall of China (left to right): Nixon; his wife, Patricia; Chinese Deputy Premier Li Hsien-nien; and Secretary of State William Rogers

of nuclear weapons. He also improved U.S.–Soviet relations through scientific and cultural exchanges.

In the November 1972 election Nixon won a landslide victory. Soon afterward a cease-fire agreement was signed with North Vietnam. North and South Vietnam went right on fighting, however, and eventually that entire country was taken over by the Communists. But American troops were out of Vietnam at last.

Also in 1973 Nixon helped bring about a cease-fire in the fighting between Israel and Egypt and Syria. This improved American prestige in the Middle East.

But while Nixon's foreign policies seemed to be working with other nations, there was serious trouble brewing at home. It started during the 1972 election campaign. Some Republicans formed a committee called the CRP, the Committee to Reelect the President. This committee hired burglars to steal secret information from the Democratic campaign headquarters in a building complex called Watergate in Washington, D.C. The burglars were caught.

At first the country paid little attention. It seemed like a stupid, third-rate theft by people of no importance. But gradually it became clear that many of the President's closest advisers had been involved. Nixon insisted that he himself had known nothing about the burglary and had no part in trying to cover it up.

More trouble came with the announcement that Vice President Spiro Agnew was officially suspected of taking bribes. This charge was never brought to court. Instead the Vice President was allowed to plead "no contest" to a charge of cheating on his income tax. (A plea of no contest is the same thing as an admission of guilt.) In October 1973, Agnew resigned as Vice President. Congressman Gerald Ford was chosen to replace him.

All this time the Watergate scandal was growing. Nixon kept insisting that he himself was not a crook. Time and again he said he had taken no part in trying to cover up the crimes committed by his associates.

But the evidence continued to build. By the spring of 1974 it seemed certain that the House of Representatives would impeach the President (or accuse him of illegal acts), and very likely that the Senate would convict him. Congress held televised hearings to investigate the scandal. Then the Supreme Court ordered Nixon to give up some secret tape recordings of talks held in his office. These tapes showed without doubt that Nixon had taken part in the coverup. He had tried to keep the FBI from investigating. He had lied repeatedly.

The country was outraged. To avoid impeachment, Richard Nixon resigned his office on August 14, 1974. Vice President Ford became President.

It was one of the most tragic moments in the history of the American presidency. Never before had a President resigned. Never before had one been so disgraced. Intelligent, well trained, with a natural instinct for politics, Nixon might have been one of the great Presidents. But he put politics above honesty. To get what he wanted he was willing to lie, and eventually he got caught.

GERALD FORD

38th President of the United States, 1974–1977

Born: July 14, 1913, in Omaha, Nebraska

Gerald Ford was born Leslie Lynch King. He was named for his father. However, his parents were divorced soon after his birth and his mother married a man named Gerald Rudolph Ford. Ford adopted his baby stepson, and the child's name was changed to Gerald R. Ford, Jr.

Gerald's new father worked for a wood-finishing company in Grand Rapids, Michigan, and it was there the boy grew up. Big and strong, he enjoyed sports. In high school he was on the football, basketball, and track teams.

Because his family had little money, Gerald usually did odd jobs like mowing lawns and washing dishes in a restaurant. His high school grades were good and he was given a one-hundred-dollar scholarship to the University of Michigan. The scholarship helped, but it could not pay all his living expenses. He waited on tables at the uni-

versity hospital and worked as a janitor. Sometimes he donated blood for money. At the same time he played center on Michigan's football team. His senior year he was named the team's most valuable player.

Ford wanted to go to law school but again money was a problem. He got a job as assistant football coach at Yale. In the off season he attended law classes. In January 1941 he received his law degree from Yale and went back to Grand Rapids to practice. Less than one year later the Japanese bombed Pearl Harbor, destroying the American fleet. The United States entered World War II, and Gerald Ford quit law to join the navy. Assigned to the light aircraft carrier *Monterey*, he saw some of the fiercest battles of the war in the Pacific.

After the war Ford returned to Grand Rapids and joined a large law firm. He also joined a number of civic organi-

Ford as a football player at the University of Michigan in 1924

zations. Cheerful and easygoing, he made many friends. In 1948 he was asked to run for Congress as a Republican. He did and was elected easily.

In the years that followed, Ford was reelected time after time, often with little opposition. His fellow congressmen liked and respected him. He served on important committees and helped investigate the murder of President Kennedy. In 1965 he was elected the leader of the Republican members of the House of Representatives.

Ford's ambition was to become the speaker of the House. But the speaker represented the majority party, and the Republicans continued to be the minority party. In 1973 Ford told his wife that it seemed unlikely he would ever become speaker. And so, he said, he would run for Congress once more, in 1974, then retire in 1976.

But in 1973 Spiro Agnew, Nixon's Vice President, was accused of taking bribes. He resigned in disgrace. And President Nixon asked Ford to become

Vice President. Ford agreed. He could still retire at the end of 1976 as he had planned.

Then President Nixon was caught in the Watergate scandal and forced to resign on August 14, 1974. Ford became the first man to be President without ever having run for the office of either President or Vice President.

Ford took office at a very troubled time in American history. President Nixon had resigned in disgrace. The war in Vietnam had ended, but in a way that many people considered a defeat for the United States. The nation was badly divided, and faith in the federal government was badly shaken.

One of Ford's first acts as President was to grant a full pardon to former President Nixon. Ford knew that without the pardon Nixon might well be brought to trial for having obstructed justice in the Watergate affair. Such a trial might go on for months, possibly years, keeping the country in turmoil. A quick pardon, Ford hoped, would end

Betty Ford welcomes Mickey Mouse and a group of children to the White House in 1974.

the matter. And Ford could get on with the job of restoring the country's self-respect. Instead, the pardon made many people angry at Ford. They felt that Nixon had committed crimes, and like any other citizen, he should have been punished.

Even so, most Americans realized that Ford himself was an honest and honorable man. His wife, Betty, became well known for speaking her own mind and championing equal rights for women. In fact, several opinion polls showed that Betty was more popular than her husband.

Ford's government was as open and simple as possible. And although he had never had any ambition to be President, he found that he enjoyed the job. He decided that rather than retire in 1976 he would run for a full term as President.

But the nation's economy was in a mess. Prices were going up almost every day. Many people were out of work. And although almost everyone respected Gerald Ford, many people wanted a President who could solve the problems of unemployment and inflation. Ford was defeated by Jimmy Carter. He retired to spend much of his time at sports such as golf and skiing.

JIMMY CARTER

39th President of the United States, 1977–1981

Born: October 1, 1924, in Plains, Georgia

Jimmy Carter's full name is James Earl Carter, Jr. But his family has always called him Jimmy. Even after he became President he still wanted to be called Jimmy.

Jimmy's father owned a farm and a small store near the little town of Plains, Georgia. Jimmy's ambition was to be a sailor. He received good grades in school and was accepted by the U.S. Naval Academy. He graduated fifty-ninth in a class of 820. Two years later he was appointed to the nuclear submarine service.

Carter was twenty-nine when his father died. He resigned from the navy and returned home to run the family farm. He became a good businessman. He enlarged the farm and bought a cotton gin and a peanut-shelling factory.

In 1954 the U.S. Supreme Court ruled that segregated schools were illegal. Many white people resented this bitterly. But Carter remembered riding to his all-white school on a school bus while black children had to walk to their all-black school. This didn't seem right to him. Hoping to work toward a just and peaceful solution to the problem, Carter ran for the county school board. He was elected. Next he ran for the state senate and was elected. Then in 1966 he ran for governor of Georgia and was defeated.

Carter kept working. He ran for governor again in 1970 and this time he won.

Outside of Georgia, Carter was practically unknown. When he first announced his candidacy for President in 1974, people made a joke of it. They asked, "Jimmy who?" Even Carter's mother was surprised. When he first told her he was going to run for President, she asked, "President of what?"

Carter worked hard campaigning for President. He traveled back and forth across the country making speeches.

Now he was helped by the fact that he was largely unknown. Many people were still angry about the Nixon presidency. The Watergate scandal had proved that the President and his close advisers were dishonest. Though Gerald Ford was an honest man, he had been chosen by Nixon to be Vice President. In many people's minds that tainted him. So when Ford ran in the 1976 presidential election, people did not want to vote for him. They wanted a President who did not belong to the Washington in-group. They wanted a newcomer.

When Carter ran against Ford, it was a close election, but Carter won.

In his inaugural address Carter called for an end to all racial discrimination. "Our commitment to human rights must be absolute," he said. And then he spoke of ". . . our ultimate goal—the elimination of all nuclear weapons from this earth."

Despite Carter's high hopes, his administration did not prove a happy one. His crusade for human rights, both at home and in other countries, angered the Soviet Union. And many people—in the United States and abroad—opposed his goal of eliminating nuclear weapons. Carter and Soviet President Leonid Brezhnev did sign a treaty (called SALT II) somewhat limiting the creation of new nuclear weapons. But the treaty was never approved by the U.S. Senate. Some senators believed it gave an unfair advantage to the Russians. During Carter's administration conflicts also arose in Latin America.

Under President Theodore Roosevelt the United States had leased the land for the Panama Canal by a combination of trickery and force. The canal passed right through Panama but it was under total U.S. control. Many

Panamanians and other Latin Americans resented this. In time this resentment grew more and more bitter.

President Carter pushed through Congress a treaty that would eventually give ownership of the canal to Panama. He realized the United States could not constantly defend the canal if the people of Panama hated and wanted to sabotage it. He believed that the good will of Latin America was worth more than technical control of the canal. He was right, but many people said Carter had "given our canal to Panama."

Carter was also blamed for the bad state of the American economy. The oil-producing countries in the Middle East raised their prices. As the price of oil continued to climb, so did the price of almost everything else. Interest rates were so high, few people could afford to borrow money to build new homes or buy new equipment. Businesses could not borrow to expand. Carter seemed uncertain about what measures to take. And the laws he did ask for were rarely passed by Congress.

To make matters worse, there was a revolution in Iran—one of America's sources of foreign oil. The old government had long been friendly to the United States, but now a group of religious militants, supported by the new Iranian government, stormed the U.S. Embassy and held American employees hostage for 444 days.

The United States refused to pay any ransom, but neither did there seem to be any way to rescue the hostages. They were held in the middle of a city by fanatics who would certainly kill them if the United States tried to rescue them by force. Carter was determined to bring them home alive, but how? When it looked as if they might be murdered anyway, Carter ordered the military to try a secret rescue. But this failed when several helicopters crashed in a desert dust storm early in the attempt. Eight marines were killed.

There was very little that Carter could do, but many people blamed him both for the economic problems and for allowing the hostages to remain imprisoned for over a year.

However, Carter did score a triumph in another part of the Middle East. Egypt and Israel had been at war, off and on, for many years. It was a dangerous situation that might explode into a larger war involving the United States and the Soviet Union. Carter invited President Anwar el-Sadat of Egypt and Premier Menachem Begin of Israel to visit him at Camp David near Washington. There the three men worked day after day with their advis-

Peanuts are what Carter grows. This shows him on his farm in Plains in 1976.

ers to draw up a fair and just peace treaty. Carter played a leading role. Called the Camp David Accord, the treaty was signed on March 26, 1979. It guaranteed peace between Israel and Egypt, and was the high point of Carter's presidency.

Carter remained unpopular in spite of this agreement and the fact that diplomats at last worked out a peaceful way for the American hostages to be released. In July 1980 an opinion poll showed that only 21 percent of the American people approved of Carter. It was the lowest rating any President had ever had in such a poll.

When Carter ran for reelection in 1980 against Ronald Reagan, he was defeated by a landslide.

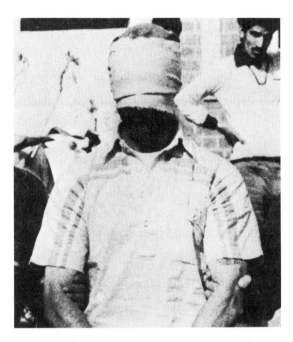

A blindfolded American hostage—one of 52 held captive in Teheran, Iran, for more than a year

Left to right: Sadat, Carter, and Begin celebrate the signing of the Camp David Accord.

RONALD REAGAN

40th President of the United States, 1981–1989

Born: February 6, 1911, in Tampico, Illinois

As a boy, Ronald Reagan lived in a number of small Illinois towns. His father was a shoe salesman and the family never had much money. Ronald liked to fish and swim and play football. He was not good at baseball because he was nearsighted and could not see the ball clearly. Later, when he got his first pair of glasses, he was surprised to learn that trees and flowers and animals had sharp, clear outlines.

Reagan went to Eureka College, a small school near his home. After college he got a job at a radio station as a sports announcer. In 1937, when he was 26 years old, he went to California to report on baseball spring training. In California a friend got him a test at a movie studio, and he was given a contract.

As a movie actor, Reagan was good but not great. He often played the role of the hero's friend—the "good guy" who helped others.

During World War II, Reagan served in the Army Air Force. He was not in combat but made training films in California. After the war he went back to Hollywood.

Up until then Reagan had been a Democrat. In fact, he would say later that until this point he had been a liberal. But now, as a member of the Screen Actors Guild, he became involved in a dispute between his union and other unions in the movie-making business. Some of the members of some of the unions had attended Communist party meetings. Reagan became convinced that Communists were trying to take over the American movie business.

Eventually the dispute among the movie labor unions was settled. But Reagan remained certain that the Soviet Union was constantly, secretly trying to destroy noncommunist governments all over the world.

Ronald Reagan was the first actor to become President. He appears here with Virginia Mayo in a scene from his 1952 movie, *She's Working Her Way Through College.*

At that point Reagan began working for the General Electric Company. It was his job to host a series of television shows. He also traveled to General Electric plants and gave speeches to the workers and the management. He was free to talk about any subject, but his basic job was to promote the good image of the company.

Most of the people that Reagan met on these tours were successful, conservative businessmen. Gradually his own political thinking became more and more conservative. He began to believe that the U.S. Government had become too big, that it interfered too much with private business.

Reagan left the Democratic party and became a Republican. When Senator Barry Goldwater ran for President against Lyndon Johnson in the 1964 election, Reagan made speeches for Goldwater. Goldwater was badly defeated, but Reagan's speeches made him very popular among the more conservative Republicans. In 1964 he was asked to run for governor of California.

At this time the war was going on in Vietnam. In California, as in the rest of the country, young people who opposed the war were staging demonstrations at universities. In his campaign Reagan promised to maintain law and order in his state. In California many people received welfare. The government gave them monthly payments because they could not support themselves. Reagan promised to prevent cheaters (people who could support themselves) from getting welfare. He also said he would reduce taxes. And he won the election easily.

Reagan served two terms as governor of California. He did not reduce taxes as he had promised, but he did force many people off welfare. Rioting at the universities gradually stopped. Most historians now agree that his record as governor was average—neither very good nor very bad.

In 1968, while still governor, Reagan tried to get the Republican nomination for President. Richard Nixon was nominated instead. In 1976 Reagan tried again, but Gerald Ford was nominated. In 1980, however, Reagan won the nomination.

At that time the country was having serious economic problems. The cost of living was going up and up. Interest rates were so high, few people could borrow money to buy new houses or cars or to start a business. Reagan promised to cut taxes and to save money by cutting government expenses. But Russian military power, Reagan said, had grown greater than that of the United States. He promised to build up the military and still save money.

A professional actor most of his life, Reagan made such convincing speeches that the newspapers called him the Great Communicator. He was elected by a wide margin over Jimmy Carter. Reagan was then 69 years old—the oldest man ever to be elected President.

As President, Reagan pushed several tax cuts through Congress. Many people said these helped the rich more than the poor. Reagan felt sure the tax cuts would improve business, which in turn would help everybody. To save money he asked Congress for heavy cuts in programs to aid the poor, the aged, the environment, and the national parks, among others. In this he was only partly successful.

At the same time he asked for and got record amounts of money for the military. Convinced of the worldwide threat of communism, he sent military advisers and millions of dollars to help defend the Central American governments of El Salvador and Honduras against rebels, and to oppose the communist-influenced government of Nicaragua. He sent U.S. troops to Lebanon. Along with small numbers of British, French, and Italian soldiers, they were supposed to act as a "peacekeeping force" in the Middle East. The international force was supposed to hold down the fighting among Israel, Lebanon, and various Arab groups. And

On a visit to Britain in 1982, Reagan tours the grounds of Windsor Castle with Queen Elizabeth II.

Reagan sent U.S. forces to invade and take over the tiny West Indian island of Grenada after its government was overthrown by communist revolutionaries.

In 1984 Reagan ran for a second term. His Democratic opponent was Walter F. Mondale, who had been Vice President under Jimmy Carter. Mondale's running mate was Representative Geraldine A. Ferraro, the first woman ever to run for Vice President on a major party ticket.

Reagan kept reminding voters that under his administration the rate of inflation had dropped sharply. Prices were still going up, but not nearly as rapidly as a few years before. Interest rates were still high, but much lower than they had been. Taxes for some people were lower. On the whole, the economy had improved.

Mondale, however, pointed to the huge amounts Reagan continued to spend on weapons while cutting back on government-sponsored programs to help the poor and the aged. Because of Reagan's increased military spending with no new taxes, the country was going deeper and deeper into debt. The 1984 federal budget deficit was estimated at more than $180 billion.

American and British soldiers search for survivors at U.S. headquarters in Beirut, Lebanon, which was bombed by terrorists in October 1983. More than 200 U.S. Marines were killed.

But Mondale's criticisms of the administration did not seem to influence the voters, and Reagan was reelected by a landslide.

Early in his second term Reagan had to go to the hospital to have a cancerous tumor removed. But he recovered quickly and began to press for funds to develop the Strategic Defense Initiative (SDI), a space-based antimissile shield to protect the U.S. against nuclear attack. The newspapers called it "Star Wars."

In addition Reagan asked Congress to rewrite the tax laws, creating a new, simplified tax system. And he met with Soviet leader Mikhail Gorbachev in Switzerland (1985) and Iceland (1986). They discussed arms reduction and cultural exchanges.

Reagan also reacted firmly to the increasing terrorist attacks around the world. In April of 1986 he ordered U.S. air strikes against military targets in Libya, after confirming that the Libyan leader, Colonel Muammar al-Qaddafi, had been behind many of the acts of terrorism directed against America.

By now Reagan was attracting a lot of attention internationally. And at home, the popularity polls gave him a 70 percent approval rating. But the Democrats gained control of the Senate—and kept control of the House—in the 1986 congressional elections.

When Reagan requested more money to support the rebel Contra forces fighting the procommunist regime in Nicaragua, Congress resisted. They thought it would mean getting involved in another Vietnam. But Reagan refused to give up. He also refused to abandon the Americans kidnapped by terrorists in Beirut. (He was sure that Iran was behind the kidnappings.)

Reagan had repeatedly stated that he would make no bargains to secure the release of hostages, so it came as a great shock when a Beirut magazine reported in November 1986 that former National Security Adviser Robert McFarlane had been in Iran negotiating an arms shipment. It was an even greater shock to learn that the arms had actually been shipped to secure the release of the kidnapped Americans. Profits from the sales had apparently been diverted to the Contras in Nicaragua.

The Iran-Contra Affair grew into a national scandal. Congress set up special committees to investigate. Reagan appointed the Tower Commission. Though the legal problems would take a long time to resolve, the initial reports criticized Reagan and his staff severely for operating outside the system of checks and balances set up by the Constitution. Later Reagan was cleared of any direct involvement, but obviously he had let his staff get out of hand.

In early October 1987 the value of U.S. stocks plunged. Reagan's financial policies were in trouble. The increased social and military spending backed by the President and Congress had resulted in huge budget deficits. The U.S. was now the biggest debtor nation in the world.

By the time Reagan left office, the stock market was performing well. People talked less about the Iran-Contra Affair and more about the dramatic "thaw" taking place in Gorbachev's Soviet Union. According to the polls, Reagan was once again one of the most popular Presidents in many years.

GEORGE BUSH

41st President of the United States, 1989–1993

Born: June 12, 1924, in Milton, Massachusetts

The election of George Bush marked the 200th anniversary of the election of George Washington, first President of the United States. Bush was also the first President since Martin Van Buren in 1836 to be elected while filling the office of Vice President.

Both of Bush's parents came from well-to-do families. He was named George Herbert Walker Bush after his maternal grandfather, George Herbert Walker. (George's mother couldn't decide whether to call her son George or Herbert so she finally used both names.) It was his grandfather Walker who established the Walker Cup, a trophy awarded every two years to the winners in team matches between American and British amateur men golfers.

George grew up in Greenwich, Connecticut, but his family spent their summers at the Walker family vacation home in Kennebunkport, Maine. There young George grew to love fishing, boating, and the sea. When he was only nine, he and his twelve-year-old brother took a boat out into the Atlantic Ocean by themselves.

In June of 1942, George was graduated from Phillips Academy, an exclusive preparatory school in Andover, Massachusetts. A few days later—on his eighteenth birthday—he went to Boston to be sworn into the U.S. Navy as a seaman second class. He wanted to be a flier in the U.S. Naval forces fighting in World War II. He received preflight training in North Carolina, and at the time he got his wings, he was the youngest pilot in the navy.

On September 2, 1944, the young flier took part in a bombing mission against Japanese bases in the Bonin Islands southeast of Japan. His TBM Avenger was launched by catapult from an aircraft carrier, but during the attack Japanese anti-aircraft guns made a direct hit on the bomber. After dropping their bombs, Bush and his two crew members had to bail out with parachutes. A U.S. submarine rescued him while he was floating on a life raft. (The other two men were never found.) For his heroism, Bush was awarded the Distinguished Flying Cross.

Fresh from his war experiences, Bush went to Yale University accompanied by his wife, Barbara, whom he had married when he returned from overseas. At Yale he majored in economics and was elected to Phi Beta Kappa, a national honor society whose members are chosen for academic achievement. In his senior year (1948) he was made captain of the Yale baseball team. During his years on the team, he earned a reputation as a good fielder and a fair hitter.

Bush has said that one of the biggest moments of his senior year came when Babe Ruth, the legendary slugger, handed Bush the original manuscript of his autobiography. The Babe was presenting it to the Yale library. George, as team captain, took part in the ceremony.

After graduation Bush moved to Texas. He wanted to get into the oil business, which was booming at that time. He joined some friends in the founding of two oil companies. One of these was an offshore oil-drilling firm of which he was president.

Although his business success had made him a millionaire, Bush began to think that he would like to go into politics. His father, Prescott Bush, had served as senator from Connecticut for ten years, beginning in 1953.

In a pre-game ceremony at Yale University in 1948, legendary slugger Babe Ruth (left) presents the manuscript of his autobiography to George Bush, captain of the Yale baseball team, for the Yale library.

For his first attempt, Bush ran as the Texas Republican candidate for the U.S. Senate in 1964, but was defeated by his Democratic opponent. Two years later he entered the race for the House of Representatives. This time he won the election as a Republican congressman from Texas, and he was reelected for a second term.

Encouraged by his success, he tried once more for the Senate in 1970. But again he lost. Soon after this second defeat, President Nixon appointed Bush as United States ambassador to the United Nations. This gave Bush his first taste of international politics. He left the post in 1973 when Nixon asked him to take over as chairman of the Republican National Committee. While he was in this post, the Watergate scandal broke (see page 135), leading to Nixon's resignation.

When Gerald Ford replaced Nixon as President, he appointed Bush to be the nation's chief diplomatic representative to China. Then in late 1975 Ford called Bush back to Washington to become director of the Central Intelligence Agency (CIA). The CIA had received a great deal of criticism for its secret activities during the Vietnam and Watergate years. Bush served as director during 1976 and 1977, striving to restore the credibility of the organization.

After Ford lost his bid for reelection, Bush decided that he would be a Republican candidate himself when the next presidential election rolled around. He made a strong start in the 1979 primary campaign but lost the nomination to Ronald Reagan. Reagan, however, chose Bush to be his running mate as Vice President, an office Bush was to fill for two terms.

Until the administration of Harry Truman, Vice Presidents had had very little to do. They presided over the Senate, but otherwise they were mostly ignored unless something happened to the President. When Franklin Roosevelt died in office during World War II, Truman complained that, as Vice President, he had had almost no knowledge of what was going on in the President's office. He recommended that in the future the Vice President be kept informed about the White House decision-making process.

When Bush became Vice President, he was given an office in the White House (the same one Jimmy Carter had set aside for *his* Vice President, Walter Mondale; Vice Presidents had not previously had an office at the White House). Bush and President Reagan had regular weekly lunch meetings. In addition, Reagan delegated many responsibilities and duties to his Vice President.

Bush's high visibility on both the national and international scenes made him the obvious candidate to succeed Reagan, and in 1988 he won the Republican nomination. He chose Dan Quayle, a senator from Indiana, as his vice presidential running mate. Bush's Democratic opponent, Michael Dukakis, was a beginner at national politics and proved to be a poor campaigner. Bush won easily.

Bush believed strongly in free trade and in continued American leadership in world affairs. He worked to set up new trade agreements that would enable foreign governments to sell their products in the United States, and American businesses to sell abroad. But generally speaking, Bush thought the federal government should do less, not more. One of the promises he made to the voters was "No new taxes."

Most of Bush's own experience in government service was in the field of foreign affairs. This turned out to be fortunate, since 1988–1992 brought dramatic developments around the globe.

The most important of these changes was the collapse of world communism. As part of his reform program, Soviet President Mikhail Gorbachev had said that the Soviet Union would no longer try to control the affairs of Eastern Europe. One by one, the communist governments of Eastern Europe were driven from power. On October 3, 1990, less than a year after the opening of the Berlin Wall, East and West Germany were reunited into one country for the first time since World War II.

At first, President Bush tried to work with Gorbachev to improve relations between the U.S. and the Soviet Union and reduce the number of nuclear weapons held by both sides. But in August of 1990, Gorbachev was driven from power. By the end of the year, the Soviet Union itself had fallen apart. Bush now had to deal with Boris Yeltsin, President of the Republic of Russia, and the leaders of the other newly independent republics.

The second major crisis of Bush's Presidency began suddenly in August of 1990. Saddam Hussein, the dictator of Iraq, invaded the tiny, oil-rich coun-

Ecstatic supporters surround George Bush in Houston, Texas, on November 8, 1988, just after learning that he has won the election in a near-landslide victory over opponent Michael Dukakis.

try of Kuwait. Bush convinced a group of nations including Britain, France, Saudi Arabia, and Egypt that it was necessary to force Hussein to withdraw his army. In February 1991, after weeks of bombing raids, the combined armies of all these nations swept across the desert and freed Kuwait.

The swift victory in the Persian Gulf war made George Bush tremendously popular. It seemed that he would win a second term easily. But problems were building up at home. Under Reagan, savings and loan associations (S&L's), a type of financial institution, had been allowed to use their depositors' money to make risky loans and investments. Since the government insures savings deposits, it had to pay back the depositors when the investments went bad and the S&L's no longer had the money. As one large S&L after another went broke, the cost to the taxpayers mounted into the billions of dollars. Bush's son, Neil, had been a director at one of the failed S&L's.

The boom of the Reagan years had ended. An economic recession, which began officially in August of 1990, proved to be the deepest in decades. Businesses went bankrupt at record rates. About ten million Americans were out of work. Moreover, during the Reagan years, the federal government had tripled the national debt. The recession made it impossible to get the budget in balance again.

Many of these problems were not really Bush's fault. The recession, for example, was worldwide. Still, when it came to dealing with troubles at home, the President seemed like a different person from the strong leader who had engineered the Gulf war. In handling foreign affairs, Bush had clear goals and stuck to them, even if it meant making controversial decisions. On the domes-

tic side, he had few bold ideas. When he did make proposals, he was often unable to get Congress to cooperate.

Many Americans were deeply worried about the rising cost of health care, but Bush proposed only minor changes to the system. His unwillingness to make defense cuts in the aftermath of the Persian Gulf war made it doubly hard to do anything about the government's rising budget deficit. As early as the summer of 1990, Bush was forced to break his promise to the voters by asking Congress to pass new taxes.

The President claimed to feel strongly about one domestic issue. He believed that abortions should be against the law. But abortion was a subject that divided supporters of both parties. Even the First Lady, Barbara Bush, said she thought abortion was a personal question, not a political one.

Campaigning for re-election in 1992, Bush faced an uphill battle. H. Ross Perot, a wealthy Texan who entered the race as an independent, focused most of his ire on Bush, criticizing him for lacking a plan to cut the national debt and promote industrial growth. Although Perot had no chance of winning himself, his attacks on Bush had an effect.

In the end, the voters decided it was time for a change. George Bush, after presiding over the end of the Cold War and an overwhelming victory in the Gulf war, was turned out of office after a single term. For the first time in sixteen years, the Democrats triumphed in a presidential race.

BILL CLINTON

42nd President of the United States, 1993–2001

Born: August 19, 1946, in Hope, Arkansas

Bill Clinton's life began with hardship and tragedy. His father, William Jefferson Blythe IV, for whom he was named, died in a car accident three months before he was born. His mother, Virginia, struggled to make ends meet. When she decided to go to nursing school, she left two-year-old Bill in her parents' care. Virginia returned home when Bill was four, and soon wed a new husband, Roger Clinton. Clinton adopted young Bill, who eventually took his name.

Though he was reunited with his mother, Bill's home life wasn't easy. Roger Clinton was an alcoholic who abused Virginia verbally and physically. Once he fired a gun during a family fight and was thrown in jail. Young Bill had to stand up to his stepfather to protect his mother.

Most people in Hot Springs, Arkansas, where Bill was raised, knew

nothing about his troubles. He never let them affect his schoolwork and he became an honors student. Bill was known for two passions: music and politics. When he wasn't practicing the saxophone, he was campaigning for so many class and club offices that his high school principal barred him from running for yet another. Nothing could put him off politics, though: Bill Clinton had already made up his mind to run for President someday. He wanted to serve his country, and he enjoyed the scramble for votes.

His 1963 election as a delegate to Boys' Nation, a national conference of high school youth, was the highlight of his teenage years. He got to travel to Washington, D.C.; visit the White House; and shake hands with his hero, President Kennedy. This brush with power made Clinton more determined than ever to

Seventeen-year-old Bill Clinton shakes hands with President John F. Kennedy at a national conference of high school students in 1963. Kennedy was one of Clinton's heroes.

become a politician. He was offered many academic and music scholarships, but chose to attend Georgetown University in Washington, D.C.—as close to the heart of American government as a student could be. At Georgetown, he majored in political science and worked as an intern for Senator William J. Fulbright, a successful politician from Arkansas and the chairman of the Senate Foreign Relations Committee. Fulbright became the young man's role model.

Clinton was a top college student. He won a prestigious Rhodes Scholarship in 1968, which sent him to Oxford University in England for two years. Heavily influenced by the civil rights and anti–Vietnam War movements of the 1960s, he felt more than ever that he wanted a political career. Upon his return to the U.S., Clinton went to Yale Law

School. Becoming a lawyer, he hoped, would be the next step to public office.

Clinton was on scholarship at Yale and worked part-time to earn extra money. In 1971, he met and fell in love with a fellow student, Hillary Rodham. They were a perfect political couple: she shared his idealism, energy, and ambition.

After graduation, Clinton went home to teach at the University of Arkansas Law School. But he didn't let much time go by before running for office. In 1974, only one year out of law school, he became a candidate for Congress. The election was close, but he lost.

Clinton wasn't discouraged. He and Rodham married in 1975, and he was elected state attorney general in 1976. Two years later, he ran for governor and won. At the age of thirty-two, he was the

Candidates took to TV talk and entertainment shows during the 1992 presidential campaign. Here Clinton, who had been offered several college scholarships in music, plays his sax on *The Arsenio Hall Show*.

youngest man at the time to hold that office. Bursting with ideas and confidence, he was determined to transform Arkansas, which was one of the poorest states in the Union. But he very quickly ran into opposition. When he raised taxes to pay for a highway-improvement program, voters got mad. Some began to distrust the young governor, who could seem arrogant and overly ambitious. Others disapproved of his lifestyle, uncomfortable with a man whose wife didn't take his name and who earned more money than he did.

The year 1980 proved to be a milestone in Clinton's life. His daughter, Chelsea, was born, and he was defeated for reelection. Though delighted by his daughter, he was also stunned by his loss.

For the first time, he began to question himself. His whole life had been dedicated to politics and public service, and now he had been turned out of office.

But it wasn't in his optimistic nature to give up. He realized he had to learn to listen to the voters. Two years later, a humbler Bill Clinton asked the people of Arkansas to give him a second chance. "I learned my lesson," he said in one interview. He won reelection and went on to become one of the country's most popular governors, attracting national attention for reforming a school system long considered one of America's worst.

In 1992, Clinton entered the presidential race as a "different kind" of Democrat, one more moderate than most of his party's candidates. He was quickly

Cheering crowds greet the winners on election night 1992. Clinton and Gore—pictured with their wives, Hillary and Tipper—represented a new generation in American leadership.

able to capture the political center. With one of his closest political advisers—his wife—campaigning at his side, he promised to invest more money in schools and job training, completely overhaul the nation's health care system, protect a woman's right to abortion, and improve the ailing economy. It was a winning formula. He and his running mate, Al Gore, triumphed over his opponent, President Bush.

On January 20, 1993, Bill Clinton was inaugurated the 42nd President of the United States. After twelve years of older Republicans, a young Democrat was in office again.

Clinton proved to be a hands-on President, a real "policy wonk." That meant he was absorbed by the details of policy and fascinated with how government worked. His belief in the power of politicians to change people's lives made Americans begin to think the country's

President Clinton attends a North American Free Trade Agreement trade fair at the White House.

153

woes could be corrected. In his first two years in office, more people of color and women were appointed to Cabinet and administrative positions than ever before. He was the first President who seemed genuinely comfortable with all kinds of minorities. He signed into law both the 1993 Family and Medical Leave Act and the 1994 Brady Handgun Violence Prevention Act. The first gave workers the right to take time off to care for sick family members or newborns. The second required a five-day waiting period for the purchase of guns, establishing a national computer network to check gun buyers' backgrounds. Most important, the economy began to recover from the recession of the past few years.

Clinton also began a significant shift in American priorities. With the Cold War over, he felt the nation's strength lay not in its military might, but in its economic clout. Though he used American troops to restore Haiti's democratically elected president to office after a military coup and sent air force planes to join in NATO's bombing of Serb positions during the Bosnian war, he believed that economic stability was the key to world peace. Touting the benefits of free trade and openly connecting foreign policy and economic policy, Clinton pushed through the 1993 North American Free Trade Agreement (NAFTA) to increase U.S. trade with Canada and Mexico.

Yet despite these victories, his administration stumbled. It was jammed with young, inexperienced professionals who

September 13, 1993, on the South Lawn of the White House:
President Clinton gestures as Israeli Prime Minister Yitzhak Rabin,
left, and Palestine Liberation Organization Chairman Yasser Arafat
shake hands after signing a peace accord.

President Clinton signs the Brady Bill on November 30, 1993, at the White House. Looking on, seated beside him, is James Brady, former Press Secretary to President Reagan who was shot during an assassination attempt on President Reagan and who, with his wife, was the bill's chief supporter.

couldn't move the wheels of government quickly. The White House seemed disorganized. Clinton himself, bright as he was, took too much time to make decisions, debating all sides of an issue and sometimes reversing his position. He paid more attention to polls than any President before him, and voters began to believe that he lacked conviction.

Clinton quickly found himself embroiled in controversy. His push to open the military to homosexuals met with fierce resistance from his own generals. The appointment of Hillary Rodham Clinton to head a task force on health care reform led some people to question whether a First Lady should have such power. They were further angered by her proposals to involve government more directly in the health care system and make health care available to all. To the

President's embarrassment, the task force's recommendations were rejected by Congress.

In 1994 came an especially heavy blow. The First Couple were accused of financial wrongdoing in a 1980s Arkansas land deal called Whitewater. A special prosecutor was appointed to investigate. The Clinton Administration seemed in disarray. By the end of 1994, voters had given Republicans control of Congress.

In 1995, political war broke out. The U.S. budget had to be balanced, but the President and Congress couldn't agree on how. Their dispute affected the funding of various government departments, and several had to be temporarily shut down. Republicans were convinced the President would buckle under such pressure, but they underestimated his distaste for some of the tax and spending cuts they proposed. By 1996, it was clear that the public blamed Congress, and not the President, for the feud. His popularity climbed, and eventually his budget was passed.

In his 1996 reelection campaign, Clinton's Republican opponent was Kansas senator Bob Dole. The economy was booming and the President seemed unbeatable. Voters didn't seem to care about Whitewater or other corruption charges made against some of his appointees. The new law he signed placing time limits on welfare was popular, despite doubts about what would happen to the poor if they couldn't find work. Most people approved of both the 1995 peace treaty ending the Bosnian war and the presence of U.S. troops in the UN peacekeeping force there. They supported the Middle East agreement signed in Washington, in which Israel granted the Palestinians limited self-rule.

Clinton won reelection handily. He used his second term to try to cement both his domestic and foreign policy accomplishments. By the end of his watch, America had had the longest economic expansion in its history, complete with the lowest unemployment rate in thirty years and the highest rate ever of new jobs created. The budget, once at a $290 billion deficit, had been balanced so successfully that Democrats and Republicans were arguing about what to do with the surplus. A credit to provide

Somalians surround a truck carrying U.S. Marines as they drive through downtown Mogadishu on a United Nations peacekeeping mission to feed the starving population.

U.S. Marines prepare their gear shortly after arrival at Sarajevo,
Bosnia-Herzegovina, December 10, 1995.

tax relief for the working poor had been expanded, and tax credits had been enacted to help families send their children to college.

An advocate of the death penalty and a tough criminal justice system, Clinton had presided over the lowest crime rate in twenty-five years. In addition, he had taken on the tobacco companies in an attempt to limit the spread of smoking, attacking their advertising campaigns that aimed at teenagers. Acknowledging his sympathy with the environmental movement, he had protected millions of acres of forest, wetlands, and desert to preserve America's wilderness, creating nine new national monuments. Under his watch, the Safe Drinking Water Act had also been expanded.

On the foreign policy front, the President had persuaded Russia to accept the expansion of NATO (North Atlantic Treaty Organization) into Eastern Europe. He'd also engineered U.S. support of China's entry into the World Trade Organization. In a major triumph for his administration, the Senate had finally removed restraints on Chinese-American trade. To foster peace, he'd helped broker the 1998 Good Friday accord in Northern Ireland, which created a national assembly where Catholics and Protestants shared power. He'd also joined with NATO in bombing Serbia to prevent Serb forces from taking over the largely Albanian region of Kosovo.

Clinton had his failures, too. Despite his efforts, there was no final resolution of the Israeli-Palestinian conflict. His attempt to make U.S. anti-missile defenses workable ended in frustration.

But what truly marked his second

term in office, and stained his legacy, was his 1998 impeachment. Clinton had been accused many times before of having sexual relationships with women outside his marriage. Now he was charged by the House of Representatives with perjury and obstruction of justice—lying under oath about an affair with a young White House intern, Monica Lewinsky, trying to cover it up, and attempting to get her to lie, too. Only the second President in American history to be impeached (the first was Andrew Johnson), he was acquitted in the Senate. The country was split in its views of Clinton. There were people who felt he had soiled the Presidency forever by behaving immorally and lying about it. They felt he had further dishonored his high office through fund-raising abuses during his 1996 campaign. Some supported the fact that investigations of his behavior continued even after the Senate acquittal, and that his right to practice law in Arkansas was under attack.

But others felt equally strongly that Clinton's private life was no one's business and that his political enemies had set him up. As proof they pointed to the fact that the President and First Lady had been cleared of all charges in the Whitewater investigation.

But it was evident to all Americans that no President since Nixon had been so tarred by scandal or ended up such a divisive figure. Only history can determine if Clinton will be remembered for that, or for his effective stewardship of America's boom years.

Chief Justice William H. Rehnquist swears in senators as jurors for
President Clinton's impeachment trial, January 7, 1999, in Washington.

President Clinton during a pause in his apology to Congress and the American people at an event in the White House Rose Garden, December 11, 1998. "I never should have misled the country, the Congress, my friends, and my family. Quite simply, I gave in to my shame . . ."

A photomontage showing the December 20, 1998, editions of newspapers with headlines of President Clinton's impeachment.

GEORGE WALKER BUSH

43rd President of the United States, 2001–

Born: July 6, 1946, in New Haven, Connecticut

First George Bush, then George W. Bush. Not since John Quincy Adams followed John Adams to the White House in 1825 has the nation elected both a father *and* a son to the Presidency. But then, the Bushes are a special family, one in which the ideal of public service has been passed from grandfather to father to son. The new President has always idolized his dad and tried to follow in his footsteps. In the 2000 presidential election, George W. had the opportunity to avenge the older man's loss to Bill Clinton by beating Al Gore. Returning his father's name to the White House carried special satisfaction for the son.

But for many years it wasn't clear that George W., the oldest Bush child, would succeed in the ways his father had. First as a boy, then as a man, he could seem more passionate about baseball than politics,

often appearing at loose ends about a career. It couldn't have been easy being born into a wealthy family and having the burden of carrying on its political legacy. "Little George," as the Bush clan called him, was born in Connecticut and moved to Texas with his parents when he was two. He grew up in the oil town of Midland and spent his summers at the family estate in Maine. He was a carefree, happy child until tragedy struck when he was seven. Robin, his younger sister, died of leukemia. The family was plunged into mourning, and George felt it was his job to take care of his mother. To distract her from her grief, he began to crack jokes and tease. Soon he developed a keen sense of humor, which has stuck with him all his life.

As the family slowly recovered, little George concentrated on what he loved

George W. Bush served in the Texas Air National Guard from 1968 to 1973.

best—athletics. He liked football, but wanted more than anything to be a baseball star like his idol, Willie Mays. There was just one problem—he couldn't hit. That didn't stop him from playing, or making himself an expert on the sport. He memorized baseball trivia and put together a huge collection of baseball cards.

Little George was a good student, and also a prankster. One day at lunchtime, in third grade, he threw a football through a school window. In fourth grade, he once came to class dressed up as Elvis Presley! He was a sociable kid—even back then he had an outgoing personality and a knack for making friends.

In 1959, the Bushes left Midland for the big city of Houston. George found himself in private school for the eighth grade. Moving homes and changing schools was a big adjustment. And two years later, George changed schools again. Starting with the tenth grade, he attended the same prestigious boarding school in Massachusetts that his father had attended.

Those weren't easy years for George. Away from home, he began to have a tough time academically. Things were so bad at first that he actually got a grade of zero on one paper. Slowly, however, the teenager grew used to his new school, helped by his energy and enthusiasm and his love of athletics. He was always on the go, playing baseball, basketball, and football, making many friends. Somehow, no matter where he was and how he felt, George understood how to get along with people. By his senior year, he was a popular guy and had suddenly become interested in conservative politics.

When George was eighteen, his father ran for the Senate. The young man returned to Texas to campaign by his side. Texas was dominated by Democrats then, and the elder Bush had an uphill race as a Republican. When his father lost, George took it hard, crying at the news. It was difficult for him to accept that the man he hero-worshiped could be defeated. His interest in politics disappeared.

In 1964, George followed family tradition and went to Yale University. A history major, he was known for both his friendliness and his awful clothes. He never did his laundry, sometimes wearing shirts and pants that he'd tossed on the floor some time before! Avoiding anything that smacked of politics, he seemed absorbed in football, flirting, and hanging out. As one friend said, "George liked, more than anything, to be with people."

Graduating in 1968, Bush wasn't sure what he should do next. He went home to

George W. Bush congressional campaign poster, circa 1978

George W. Bush's 1978 congressional campaign takes him to talk with workers in the Midland oil fields of west Texas.

Houston, where he worked for friends of his father, but never held down a job for long. The Vietnam War was raging, but Bush chose not to enlist. Instead he joined the Texas Air National Guard, learning to be a fighter pilot like his father. When he wasn't in the air, he could often be found racing around the city in his sports car. A fun-loving guy, he led an active social life. As Bush himself said of those years, "I had no responsibilities whatsoever." One former boss said, "He was searching for what to do."

Then once again, politics captured his interest. Though tempted to run for office, he didn't know where to start. So he began to school himself in the art of campaigning. In 1970, he helped his father when the older Bush ran again for the Senate (he lost). Then in 1972, he worked on another Senate campaign, this one for a friend of his father's.

By 1973, Bush felt the need to settle on a career. His application to the University of Texas Law School was rejected, but the Harvard Business School accepted him. Determined to take advantage of this opportunity, he studied hard and earned a master's in business administration in 1975.

Like his father before him, Bush found himself in Midland with the idea of starting an oil business. One friend said, "He was focused on proving himself to his dad." He made good use of Bush senior's connections and his own winning personality to convince people to invest in his company. Absorbed in his quest for a big oil strike, he didn't pay much attention to the routines of daily

George W. and Laura Bush with their two daughters in Kennebunkport, Maine, 1990

life. Often dressing sloppily, he wore clothes that didn't match. When the frame of his bed broke, he tied it together with a necktie. What he did manage to keep up was his active social life, and he frequently hung out with friends, chewing tobacco and drinking beer.

Despite his best efforts, Bush's oil business struggled. So in 1977, he decided to make the leap into politics and run for Congress. Because of his father, the Bush name was well known in Texas, and the son was convinced that the time had come to make his own contribution to the family tradition.

But before the campaign got under way, an event occurred that changed his life. In the summer of 1977, Bush went to a barbecue thrown by friends and was introduced to Laura Welch, a quiet, confident librarian whom he'd attended grade school with. It was love at first sight. The attractive Laura laughed at his jokes and listened as he talked. Her intelligence and calm smoothed out his boyish impatience and pulled him into a newfound maturity. As his mother declared, "He was struck by lightning when he met her." A few months later, the two were married.

There was no time for a honeymoon, however. "Bushie," as his wife called him, plunged right into his campaign. Only thirty-one, he was a tireless candidate.

But his energy couldn't make up for his inexperience. His opponent was able to label him an overconfident outsider whose only qualification was his father's name. Bush himself sometimes came across as arrogant on the campaign trail. When he lost soundly, he realized he had a lot to learn. "Defeat humbles you," he said later. "Frankly, getting whipped was probably a pretty good thing for me."

He returned to his oil business and, despite his failure to find a major strike, seemed happy with his life. His father was elected Vice President in 1980, and he was very proud. Then in 1981, he and his wife had twin daughters, on whom he doted.

Yet as the years passed, Bush's lack of business and political success began to affect him. He started to drink heavily.

Always temperamental, he could be irritable and loud. Although he didn't mean to, he sometimes offended people. As one cousin said, he seemed "on the road to nowhere at the age of forty."

His wife grew increasingly disturbed by his behavior. Eventually, she threatened to leave him if he didn't stop drinking. Bush didn't want to lose her and their daughters, nor could he stand the idea that he might end up embarrassing his father.

In 1985, his parents arranged for him to meet with Billy Graham, the famous evangelical preacher. After that encounter, something inside Bush started to change. He developed a strong religious faith and began reading the Bible every day. Then in 1986, after showing up

George W. Bush and his father, former President George Bush, in the locker room of the Texas Rangers with sports broadcaster Joe Morgan on April 8, 1981

drunk at his fortieth birthday celebration, he vowed to quit drinking—and did. He also gave up smoking and chewing tobacco.

George W. was fit and ready to help when his father decided to run for President. In 1987, the son moved to Washington to serve as a senior adviser to the campaign. After his dad's victory in 1988, he was a key member of the team that recommended appointments to office.

Upon his return to Texas, Bush came face to face with his own political ambitions. But the time didn't seem right yet for another run for office. Somehow he had to prove to voters that he wasn't merely his father's son. There had to be a way to demonstrate that he had the character and know-how to make government work.

In an inspired move, Bush came up with the perfect idea. He'd make his boyhood baseball dreams come true and get his name in headlines all over Texas. Together with a group of partners, he bought the major-league Texas Rangers in 1989. With his name linked to a Texas team, no one could ever accuse him of being an outsider again.

Under his leadership, the Rangers had success after success, including the opening of a new ballpark. Bush was often in the news, not merely as a team owner but also as an effective businessman. His reputation grew, and the Republican Party began to consider him as a candidate for governor. When Bush senior ran for reelection in 1992, Bush junior took time out from his own career to again help his father.

It was Bill Clinton's year, however, and the elder Bush was defeated. George W. knew that it was now up to him to keep

Texas governor George W. Bush and wife, Laura, at a rally in Des Moines, Iowa, January 24, 2000

Texas governor George W. Bush addresses the delegates at the Republican National Convention in Philadelphia on August 3, 2000.

the family's name in the political spotlight.

So in 1994, he ran for governor of Texas against the tough Democratic incumbent, Ann Richards. Wearing cowboy boots with the Texas flag or GOD BLESS AMERICA emblazoned on them, Bush promised a broad tax cut for Texans, along with education reform. He used his good looks, sharp wit, and talent for connecting with people to get the voters' attention. They liked his message of limited government and respect for individual rights.

At the age of forty-eight, Bush won his first election. The family torch had been passed to a new generation. He gave up his shares in the Rangers and moved into the governor's mansion. George W. had finally come into his own.

He was an immensely popular gover-

nor. Even his political opponents liked him. So energetic and talkative that some of his staff nicknamed him "the Energizer Bunny," he was able to get many of his programs enacted. As promised, he cut taxes, improved the state literacy rate, and began to reform the public schools. Guided by his belief in a strong criminal justice system, he enforced the death penalty more than any Texas governor before him.

Heady with success, he began to consider running for national office. But he knew that no one would take him seriously unless he won reelection and won big. In the state's history, no other Texas governor had been elected to consecutive four-year terms. In 1998, he faced the voters again—and coasted to victory, taking a whopping 68.6 percent of the vote.

There was just one more hurdle to the

Republican presidential candidate George W. Bush during a campaign stop in New Mexico on August 19, 2000

Republican presidential nomination. In 2000, Bush faced a well-respected opponent, Senator John McCain, in a series of tough primary contests. But his conservative record and pro-life stance stood him in good stead, and he was able to beat back the challenge. After just five years as an elected official, he secured the nomination.

Now the White House beckoned. But

President-elect Bush after he addressed the nation from the Texas House of Representatives in Austin, Texas, on December 13, 2000

first Bush would have to beat Bill Clinton's Vice President, Al Gore, the Democratic nominee. It would be a pleasure to turn those who had helped defeat his father out of office. Though Gore tried to label him as inexperienced and accused him of representing the interests of the rich, Bush worked hard to convince voters that he was a "compassionate conservative" of unquestioned character. He offered Americans a vision of a limited government that gave its citizens a choice of where to send their children to school, how to invest their Social Security money, and how to best insure their health.

In the closest race of modern times, Bush lost the popular vote but became President when the state of Florida gave him an Electoral College majority. The election was bitter and remained undecided for more than five weeks. In the end, it was the courts, including the

Supreme Court in a 5–4 decision, that upheld his 537-vote Florida margin, marking the first time in American history that judges determined the outcome of a presidential election.

The Bush Presidency won't be that different from the Bush governorship. Never fond of legislative detail, he's a man who emphasizes the big picture. Self-confident despite being a minority President, he's surrounded himself with many of his father's old appointees and advisers. With his relaxed style, he won't give up his sense of fun. "I have always looked for the lighter side of life," he once said. Still very much the baseball fan, he keeps up a memorabilia collection that includes over 250 autographed baseballs!

Most of all, he rests happily in the knowledge that the Bush political legacy is alive and well. He'd said before, "I kind of figure life is going to work its way out somehow," and he turned out to be right.

THE 2000 ELECTION

The 2000 presidential election was the closest and most complicated of the modern era. The margin was so narrow that, for the first time in American history, the candidates fought a legal battle to determine the outcome. Disputes about one state's vote count became so tangled that no winner could be confirmed until the Supreme Court stepped in. But the justices were sharply divided, and it was only by a 5–4 decision that the contest was finally resolved.

The election turned on the state of Florida and its twenty-five electoral votes. When the Republican candidate, Governor George W. Bush of Texas, won there by a mere 537 ballots out of just over six million cast, the victory gave him a slim majority in the all-important Electoral College. It is this poorly understood institution that actually elects the President.

Bush went to the White House even though the Democratic candidate, Vice President Al Gore, Jr., won the national popular vote by over 300,000 ballots. Thus, the 2000 election was the fourth time in American history that a minority President—a candidate who loses the popular vote but triumphs in the Electoral College—took office.

The country had gone to the polls as usual on Election Day, November 7, 2000, but there was no clear winner until five weeks later. The trouble started early. Shortly before 8:00 p.m. Eastern Standard Time, the television networks declared that Florida's electoral votes had gone to Gore; hours later, they moved them to the Governor's column, naming Bush the President-elect. Gore was actually in a limousine on the way to deliver his concession speech when Bush's margin of victory appeared to shrink below 300 votes. With a lead that small, state law required a recount. All of a sudden, Florida was too close to call.

Gore turned around. He wasn't going to concede yet. Neither he nor Bush could be President without winning the state. It took 270 votes to be an Electoral College victor. Gore had 267, Bush 246. The election was far from over.

A recount by machine confirmed that Bush was on top, and was followed by an absentee ballot tally that increased his lead to 930 (absentee ballots are cast by voters who—for a variety of reasons—are unable to come to the polling place: they may be disabled, for instance, or temporarily living out of state). At the

A passerby reads the headline of the *Indianapolis Star* on a street corner on November 8, 2000.

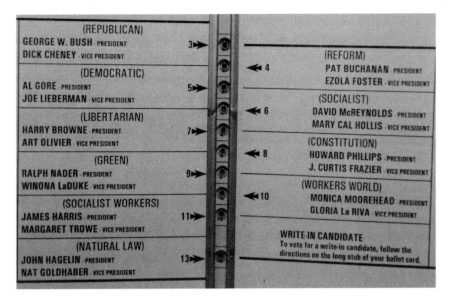

The "butterfly" ballot used in the 2000 presidential
election in Palm Beach County, Florida

same time, recounts by hand got under way in key Democratic counties, which had the potential to tip the scales in Gore's favor. It was these manual recounts that triggered complex legal and political maneuvering, with both parties filing lawsuits in local, state, and federal courts. These lawsuits, mostly won by the Republicans, ultimately decided the election.

In and out of court, the Gore and Bush teams argued about a rash of issues. Many Democrats believed Gore was cheated out of thousands of votes because, among other reasons, one county issued confusing voting instructions and another used a poorly designed "butterfly" ballot. Republicans complained that hundreds of absentee ballots—many from military personnel—were unfairly disqualified. Democrats objected that ballot applications in two counties had been illegally filled out. There was also a furious debate about the motives of Florida's Secretary of State, Katherine Harris. She interpreted state law as imposing a deadline on recounts and ended up certifying Bush the winner of

Florida before the recounts were finished.

As the vote was counted, recounted, and counted again, controversy swirled around Florida's voting system itself. The state used paper ballots requiring people to punch out little bits of paper, called chads, next to a candidate's name. Democrats insisted that machines couldn't accurately tally such ballots since chads sometimes don't fall out, even when punched. They charged that not every vote would count unless the ballots were examined by hand. Republicans argued that when chads don't fall out, there's no way of knowing the voter's intent. A recount by hand, they stated, would be flawed by human error and subject to fraud. Given such a fundamental disagreement, it was no wonder that the recount soon became clouded by charges and countercharges of cheating.

But the dispute between the candidates that proved most decisive focused on the Florida Supreme Court. There was a legal deadline of December 12, by which all states had to select their electors or risk forfeiting the right to cast their votes in the Electoral College. As that deadline neared, the court issued a last-minute order to all county election officials: count every undervote (a ballot that a machine can't read). The Bush forces immediately appealed to the U.S. Supreme Court, contending that the Florida judges had overreached their authority. Only the state legislature, they insisted, could make the kind of election law changes that the court's order involved. But even more, Bush's lawyers maintained, the recount itself was unfair since the court had not established one statewide standard for every Florida county to decide which ballots were legitimate.

The Supreme Court divided along conservative/liberal lines. It granted the Republicans a stay—a halt to the recount. Then, three days after both parties presented their cases, the justices voted 5–4 to declare the Florida Supreme Court's order unconstitutional and cancel the recount.

Their verdict gave the election to Bush. Yet even then there were millions of Americans who continued to believe that it was Gore who'd actually won. Not since 1876 had a presidential election been so controversial.

The 2000 election crisis all came about because of the Electoral College. In 2000, Americans were once again reminded that they don't directly choose their President. The Constitution gives that power to electors—men and women appointed in each state every four years who make up the Electoral College. When citizens vote, they actually cast their ballots not for the candidates whose names appear in the voting booth, but for one party or another's slate of electors. By tradition, these electors support the candidate who wins the most votes in their state, but legally they are not required to

do so. Congress officially tallies all the electors' votes, but may reject those votes it deems suspicious (the result of cheating or trickery).

The makeup of the Electoral College is a direct reflection of the population of each state. The number of a state's electors is the total of how many Senators and Representatives it has. Thus, the most populous states have the most electoral votes. But the system has a built-in guarantee of power for every state: since each has at least three electoral votes, even the tiniest has the ability to influence the election. That's because to become President, a candidate must win a majority of the electors' votes and not the most ballots cast nationwide. If no candidate wins a majority, the House of Representatives elects the President.

Many historians feel that the Founding Fathers established the Electoral College because they trusted neither the politicians nor the people. During the Constitutional Convention of 1787, the Founding Fathers engaged in a weeks-long debate about how a President should be elected. Congress shouldn't do it, they agreed, and neither should the state legislatures, since a chief executive put in office by politicians would owe those politicians favors. Yet the people themselves couldn't do it: a national vote would give the most populated states an unfair advantage, and could also lead to chaos and mob rule.

Their solution was to create the Electoral College. It was a compromise that has sometimes led to political crisis. In 1824, 1876, and 1888, the people elected one man and the Electoral College another. In all three instances, the minority Presidents oversaw unpopular administrations and were single-term Presidents.

Demonstrators jam the sidewalk in front of the U.S. Supreme Court, December 11, 2000, in Washington, D.C.

In 1824, Americans elected Andrew Jackson over John Quincy Adams, but the third-party candidacy of Henry Clay prevented Jackson from winning an electoral-vote majority. The contest was thrown to the House of Representatives, which voted Adams the Presidency.

In 1876, Democratic candidate Samuel Tilden won the popular vote yet was defeated by Republican Rutherford B. Hayes. That's because electoral votes from three states fell into dispute, and a Republican Congress appointed a special commission to investigate. Stacked in favor of the Republicans, the commission awarded Hayes all the disputed votes, giving him a one-vote majority in the Electoral College and the Presidency. The political shenanigans behind this election were so apparent to the nation that Hayes was forevermore known as "Rutherfraud."

The 1888 election was, by contrast, clean. Republican Benjamin Harrison ran against Democrat Grover Cleveland and lost the popular vote to him. Nonetheless, Harrison became President when he won an Electoral College majority.

In 2000, Bush won an election some felt was the result of a flawed voting system. Others suspected that his Electoral College victory was due in part to the control of Florida by his party. The prolonged recount process came to a bitter end for Democrats, many of whom remained convinced that the Supreme Court had acted improperly. Nonetheless, Vice President Gore and President-elect Bush urged the parties to come together for the good of the nation.

Polls showed that 80 percent of Americans accepted Bush as the legitimate winner of the election. Still, lingering doubts center on the Electoral College. Should the winner of the popular vote go home and the loser move into the White House? Or should the Founding Fathers have the last word? Their system has, after all, guaranteed U.S. democracy for over two hundred years. One thing's certain: the Electoral College will dominate debate about the Presidency for many years to come.

Index

Page numbers in *italics* refer to illustrations.

Also available in this series . . .

The Look-It-Up Book of

FIRST LADIES

With a foreword by former First Lady Rosalynn Carter

Includes results of the 2000 election!

by S.A.Kramer

Includes a chapter on First Lady Laura Bush!